LIST OF TITLES

Already published

In preparation

OUTLINE STUDIES IN BIOLOGY

Editor's Foreword

The student of biological science in his final years as an undergraduate and his first years as a graduate is expected to gain some familiarity with current research at the frontiers of his discipline. New research work is published in a perplexing diversity of publications and is inevitably concerned with the minutiae of the subject. The sheer number of research journals and papers also causes confusion and difficulties of assimilation. Review articles usually presuppose a background knowledge of the field and are inevitably rather restricted in scope. There is thus a need for short but authoritative introductions to those areas of modern biological research which are either not dealt with in standard introductory textbooks or are not dealt with in sufficient detail to enable the student to go on from them to read scholarly reviews with profit. This series of books is designed to satisfy this need. The authors have been asked to produce a brief outline of their subject assuming that their readers will have read and remembered much of standard introductory textbook on biology. This outline then sets out to provide by building on this basis, the conceptual framework within which modern research work is progressing and aims to give the reader an indication of the problems, both conceptual and practical, which must be overcome if progress is to be maintained. We hope that students will go on to read the more detailed reviews and articles to which reference is made with a greater insight and understanding of how they fit into the overall scheme of modern research effort and may thus be helped to choose where to make their own contribution to this effort. These books are guidebooks, not textbooks. Modern research pays scant regard for the academic divisions into which biological teaching and introductory textbooks must, to a certain extent, be divided. We have thus concentrated in this series on providing guides to those areas which fall between, or which involve, several different academic disciplines. It is here that the gap between the textbook and the research paper is widest and where the need for guidance is greatest. In so doing we hope to have extended or supplemented but not supplanted main texts, and to have given students assistance in seeing how modern biological research is progressing, while at the same time providing a foundation for self help in the achievement of successful examination results.

Metals in Biochemistry

P.M. Harrison

Professor, Department of Biochemistry
University of Sheffield

R.J. Hoare

University of Sheffield Medical School

1980

London and New York

Chapman and Hall

150th Anniversary

First published in 1980 by
Chapman and Hall Ltd
11 New Fetter Lane, London EC4P 4EE
Published in the USA by
Chapman and Hall
in association with Methuen, Inc.
733 Third Avenue, New York, NY 10017
© *1980 P. M. Harrison and R. J. Hoare*

Printed and bound in the
United States of America

ISBN 0 412 13160 9

British Library Cataloguing in Publication Data

Harrison, PM
    Metals in biochemistry. - (Outline
    studies in biology).
    1. Metals in the body
    2. Metals - Physiological effect
    I. Title   II. Hoare, RJ
    III. Series
    574.1'9214   QP532   79-41813

    ISBN 0-412-13160-9

Contents

Preface

In this book we present a largely biochemical look at the metals of life and their functions, which we hope will be of interest to chemists and biologists as well as biochemists. The field of 'inorganic biochemistry' is one of rapid change. Recent developments in our knowledge of the activity of calcium, and of the iron–sulphur proteins, are two examples, and increasing attention is being paid to non-metals as well [3].

For reasons of space, we shall restrict ourselves to the normal biological activities of metals. We must ignore, on the one hand, the gross physiological effects of metal deficiency or toxicity, and on the other, the many model studies which have been stimulated by the unusual properties of metals in biological systems. Usually the synthesis of model metal compounds follows rather than anticipates the discovery of novel biological configurations. However, such studies give us a firm basis for an understanding of the biological systems, and sometimes answer questions that cannot be tackled any other way (for instance, what is the net charge on an iron–sulphur cluster?). As a result, we can refer to new and interesting information on the metals of life at a chemical level.

We gratefully acknowledge the help of Professor P. Banks and Dr D. Fenton who have read and criticized the manuscript, though any errors or misconceptions remain our own responsibility. We thank Mr P. Elliot for preparing Fig. 5.2.

Richard J. Hoare
Sheffield, 1979   Pauline M. Harrison

Textual conventions

Conventional abbreviations are used to refer to amino-acids as residues in protein chains, or to their side-chains as ligands co-ordinating metal ions:

HIS	(either ring N)	THR ⎱ (hydroxyl O)	
GLU ⎱ (carboxylate anion)		SER ⎰	
ASP ⎰		LYS	(amino N)
ASN	(amide carbonyl O)	CYS	(thiolate anion)
MET	(S)		

Intracellular and extracellular concentrations of ions are referred to by the subscripts i and e respectively, as in $[Na^+]_e$.

1 The essential metals and their evolution

Living organisms have many different requirements for metals. Some are for small amounts of an ion bound in a specialized site, while others are for 'bulk' quantities in solution, at millimolar or greater concentrations. In this chapter we shall start by looking at these requirements, and then consider how they may reflect the course of early biochemical evolution.

We can define two bulk roles for metals: maintaining osmotic balance, and providing a general cationic environment. Although cells (e.g. in plants) can protect themselves against swelling and lysis in hypotonic media by means of inextensible cell walls, they cannot survive collapse in hypertonic fluids. Osmotic pressure inside the cell must at least match that outside. As intracellular organic molecules are predominantly anionic, metal cations are important both for osmotic and electrical charge balance. They also serve in the maintenance and reversal of transmembrane electrical potentials. The metals involved in these roles, from groups IA and IIA of the Periodic Table, we can call the major metals – they are also the major cations found in sea water (Table 1.1).

On the other hand, specific physiological requirements are known for at least twenty-seven elements (Table 1.2), including the major metals (K, Mg, Na, Ca), six generally required minor metals (Mn, Fe, Co, Cu, Zn, Mo), and five other metals which are required in trace amounts by at least some organisms (V, Cr, Sn, Ni, Al). The list will undoubtedly grow as experimental techniques improve. Our ultimate aim is to express metal activities in biochemical terms.

Table 1.1 The essential elements of life, and their abundances in the ocean (mM)

Major elements		Minor elements		(continued)	
C,H,N,O*		B	0.426	Se	0.000 051
Cl	536	Si	0.107[†]	Cu*	0.000 047
Na	456	F	0.068	V	0.000 039
Mg*	56	Cr	0.000 96	Mn*	0.000 036
S*(SO_4^{2-})	28	I	0.000 47	Ni (*)	0.000 036
Ca	10	Al	0.000 37	Sn	0.000 025
K*	9.7	Fe*	0.000 18[†]	Co*	0.000 008
P*(HPO_4^{2-})	0.001	Zn*	0.000 16	Pb(?)	0.000 0001
		Mo*	0.000 104		

Notes: *Element generally required [21]. [†]Values can vary between water masses by a factor of 1000.

How far can we explain the specificity of these requirements? One answer is that among the metals available to living things, some have unique chemical properties which give them unique roles. Calcium and molybdenum particularly spring to mind in this context, both with highly distinctive physiological roles. Another answer is that biological binding sites, especially high affinity ones, are tailored to suit one particular metal, and no other. (We shall touch on both these factors in later chapters.) Metalloproteins with redox functions are especially demanding in metal specificity, but often there seems little reason why a different metal bound to a different protein might not serve an identical biochemical purpose. Copper proteins can mimic iron proteins in almost all their varied functions at a chemical level (Chapters 3 and 4), yet when we look at the redox systems of photosynthesis and oxidative phosphorylation, we find an almost total dependence on iron. The explanation may be in part historic, involving not only the suitability and availability of a metal, but the evolution of a protein to bind it and interact with other molecules as required, and also the metabolism (transport processes etc.) to deliver it to its binding site.

We assume that many biochemical roles both for minerals and organic compounds evolved when such molecules were abundant. If they became less available, cells developed appropriate mechanisms to accumulate them, by concentration or biosynthesis. Past environmental abundance is, therefore, a further possible determinant of present-day specificities for metal ions, and using information from chemical, fossil and geological studies, it is possible to throw some light on this evolutionary aspect of metal physiology.

1.1 The major metals

In all living cells we find a major requirement for potassium and magnesium, which serve as counter-ions for the various macromolecules, and stabilize their structures. K^+ is the principal cation mediating osmotic balance with the external medium, and it is accumulated in concert with the expulsion of Na^+ (Table 1.2). In animals, this Na^+/K^+ separation has allowed the evolution of the reversible trans-membrane electrical potentials essential for nerve and muscle action. The muscle cells of different animals have an optimal $[K^+]_i$ of $160\,mM \pm 40\,mM$. This is not exceeded even in marine animals whose internal fluids approach the osmolarity of sea water, and possibly corresponds to the region of stabilization of the specialized muscle proteins. In nerve, on the other hand, increased $[K^+]_i$ permits larger electrical potentials and internal ionic conductance. Here $[K^+]_i$ is limited by the overall osmolarity ($[K^+]_i \leq [Na^+]_e$, since Na^+ is the principal external cation), and exceeds 300mM in squid axoplasm.

Magnesium is accumulated in lesser quantities than potassium, but is equally vital, especially in stabilizing or activating intracellular phosphates. These include nucleic acids as well as small molecules

Table 1.2 Major ion concentrations in living systems (mM)

	K^+	Mg^{2+}	Na^+	Ca^{2+}
Extreme halophiles				
Halobacterium salinarium*	4570		1370	
Required medium	> 2	> 150	4600	
Marine organisms				
Squid axoplasm	344	10	65	0.05
Giant alga: vacuole	625		44	
cytoplasm	434		40	
Sea water	10	56	456	10
Plants, freshwater organisms, miscellaneous				
Giant alga: vacuole	80		26	
cytoplasm	125		5	
Required medium	0.1		0.2	
E. coli*	250	20	50	5
Euglena*	103	5	5	0.3
Yeast (dry)*	111	13	10	1
Human blood				
Erythrocytes	155	2.7	21	$< 10^{-4}$
Plasma	4.1	1.1	141	2.4

Notes: These data are illustrative of the very wide variations of composition found in living cells. Concentrations are millimolar except *mmol kg^{-1}.

and phospholipids in the cell membrane. Other roles include the stabilization of ribosome and microtubule structure.

Although sodium and calcium have a number of specific roles both within and without the cells of many organisms, only higher animals have a universal requirement for sodium, as a bulk cation in their internal fluids. Together with Ca^{2+} and K^+, Na^+ is an agent of the transmission of action potentials in excitable tissue.

Outside the animal kingdom, a trace requirement for calcium is general in plants and algae, and occasional in fungi and bacteria. As in animals, it is used in extracellular mineralization, for instance in the surface coccoliths of certain algae. The presence of sodium and calcium in micro-organisms may only indicate that their growth is limited by some factor: in growth these metals will be expelled and potassium and magnesium accumulated.

1.2 The minor metals

Of the minor metals, six are generally required by most forms of life, and can be demonstrated as enzyme co-factors – iron, copper, manganese, cobalt, zinc and molybdenum. Cobalt, as vitamin B_{12}, is generally required by micro-organisms and animals, while higher plants also require free cobalt. Manganese activates many enzymes *in vitro*, but because it does not bind strongly to most of them, its specific chemistry *in vivo* is difficult to verify. A *prima facie* case can also be made for a general requirement for nickel. It is involved in bacterial carbon dioxide fixation, activates a plant urease, is essential for chick development, and is transported in mammalian plasma by a specific protein.

9

The remaining minor metals are not (yet) known to be generally required, and some may only have been adopted by higher forms of life. Vanadium is required by green algae, yeasts, and (like tin and chromium) rats – all eucaryotes. A chromium-containing 'glucose tolerance factor' of mol wt 3–500, found in meats, grains and certain yeasts, is involved in the control of glucose metabolism by insulin in animals. Aluminium is required by maize, and there are indications of a lead requirement in rats! The experimental difficulty in establishing such requirements is that living organisms are adept at accumulating trace elements from media of extreme dilution, even from impurities in chemicals, airborne dust, or leachings from vessel walls.

However, mere accumulation, or even metabolism, of a metal does not establish a physiological need. Certain plants absorb nickel up to 25% ashed weight, while marine organisms are known with high contents of titanium, vanadium, chromium, niobium and thallium. It is hard to believe that all these represent biological requirements. The mammalian metabolism of cadmium appears to be a detoxification mechanism, and the same is true of the notorious bacterial methylation of mercury.

1.3 Metals and early biochemical evolution

The origin of life is one of the most intriguing problems in biology. In rocks dating back 2.6 and possibly 3.3 out of the 4.5 billion years of the Earth's history, the forms of micro-organisms resembling blue-green algae have been identified, and also 'chemical fossils' (probably of biological origin) such as n-alkanes, isoprenoids, porphyrins, and possibly amino-acids. Life was already biochemically quite advanced, though phylogenetically primitive.

To delve further back into the process of biochemical evolution is a question of inference, based on two approaches. The first is the study of extant species which may have changed little since the early days. One can study such 'primitive' organisms by comparing protein form and sequence, and measuring DNA-relatedness between species. It has been assumed, for instance, that the photosynthetic and chemi-autotrophic bacteria are descended from the survivors of early forms of life which never adapted to oxygen in the atmosphere. It may be that combined studies on ferredoxin, rubredoxin and flavodoxin sequences will lead to an evolutionary tree for bacteria similar to that provided by cytochrome c and haemoglobin for higher forms of life.

The second approach is speculation about the Earth's primeval environment, with theoretical and practical studies on the chemistry that may have developed therein, including consideration of the available metal ions. The nature of the Earth's early atmosphere, initially emitted from its interior, is controversial [24], but is generally agreed to have been chemically reducing and to have contained no oxygen. It may have resembled present-day volcanic gas (nitrogen, carbon dioxide, a few percent hydrogen and other trace gases), or a more reducing mixture including much methane and ammonia. Natural energetic processes (ultraviolet radiation, volcanoes, lightning, radio-activity, etc.) and the exposure of reactive or catalytic minerals led to the formation of organic compounds amongst which heterotrophic life developed. Experiments based on such ideas in simulated 'prebiotic' conditions have yielded such compounds as amino-acids, nitrogen bases and porphyrins. There is also evidence that stable bases like porphyrins have arrived with the organic material in meteorites. Porphyrins and iron can spontaneously form haem.

Probably from the beginning, the surface of the earth was becoming more oxidized, as a result of the atmospheric photolysis of water and steady gravitational loss of hydrogen into space, and the continued burial of reduced carbon compounds in the ocean sediments. As photosynthetic organisms started to liberate oxygen, reducing compounds in the ocean and atmosphere largely disappeared, and over a period of perhaps 2.5 to 1.8 billion years ago, the atmosphere changed from anoxic to oxygenic. Two of the profound results of this change were as follows. First, living cells had to develop aerobic biochemistry, or seek out the remaining anaerobic niches. Second, the ozone layer of the atmosphere built up, shielding off the Sun's ultraviolet radiation, and allowing life to move to progressively shallower water, and eventually to colonize land.

In addition, the mineral environment would have been affected, with progressive oxidation of certain elements. Calculations along these lines [2] have led to a proposed sequence of changes in the solubility, and hence availability, of metal ions. The broad pattern for transition metals is as follows. Initially (i.e. at the lowest environmental redox potential envisaged, $-325\,mV$), most iron would have formed Fe_3O_4, and the ocean would have contained up to $0.2\,mM$ Fe^{2+}. Sulphur would have been present in iron sediments as ferrous sulphide, pyrites (FeS_2) or pyrrhotite ($Fe_{0.86}S$). Manganese would have been abundant, perhaps $50\,mM$. Molybdenum would have formed sulphide deposits, mixed with iron, or as molybdite (MoS_2). Copper would have been in the form of highly insoluble cuprous sulphides, from which it would not have been released until sulphide became oxidized. (This probably also applies to cobalt and zinc.) Thereafter, cuprous complexes of thiols and amines, and eventually Cu^{2+}, would have appeared in solution. With further increase of oxidation level, Fe^{2+} and Mn^{2+} would have become oxidized and precipitated as FeOOH and MnO_2, and their oceanic concentrations would have dropped to their present low levels. (The deposition of Fe^{3+} in banded ironstones 3.75 billion years ago puts an early date on iron precipitation, though it does not prove biological activity.) All these changes would have preceded the actual appearance of oxygen in the atmosphere.

Alkaline and alkaline earth metals are only indirectly affected by changing oxidative levels in the environment. Their concentrations are controlled by equilibration with quartz and aluminosilicates, and have probably not altered much.

How can we relate these changing patterns of soluble metals in the environment to the origin and evolution of life? We need not doubt, from our knowledge of the reactivity of co-ordinated ligands, that prebiotic chemical reactions will have been assisted and perhaps shaped by metal-ion catalysis. The formation of reduced porphyrins from pyrroles around a divalent metal ion is one example. Carbon compounds in the ocean at large may have been too dilute for early biochemical development, and it is likely that this took place in more specialized sites, such as tidal pools, possibly with mineral surfaces playing an important part. An abundance of Mg^{2+}, with its high charge/radius ratio, probably had a great influence, and today the ion supports many fundamental cell processes.

Both free Fe^{2+} and ferrous sulphide were available to early life. With such material, the redox proteins ferredoxin and rubredoxin can assemble spontaneously from their apoproteins. For this and other reasons it is possible that bacterial ferredoxin was one of the earliest conjugated proteins. Ferredoxin has roles associated with fermentation, photosynthesis, and the metabolism of hydrogen gas. The abiotic formation of porphyrins and haem has already been mentioned. Cytochromes may, therefore, have also developed quite early on, and together with manganese and a magnesium porphyrin (chlorophyll), provided the catalysts for photosynthesis.

We can speculate on the early course of evolution in terms of a succession of chemical crises. Fermentation of prebiotic compounds by early cells led to the loss of metabolizable substrates, and the liberation of carbon dioxide and hydrogen or reduced carbon compounds. Photosynthesis provided a means of reversing this process, but the gradual loss of reduced compounds to sediment meant that inorganic sources of reducing power had to be exploited. Eventually ammonia and sulphide were converted to nitrate, dinitrogen and sulphate, and means had to be devised to regain nitrogen and sulphur from their oxidized forms for synthetic purposes. We may assume that molybdenum had already appeared on the chemical scene at this point, as today it is uniquely essential for the enzymatic reduction of nitrate, dinitrogen and sulphite.

The next great crisis occurred when the blue-green algae or their ancestors developed the abstraction of electrons from water, as other sources of reducing power for photosynthesis had disappeared. This lead to the appearance of oxygen. Oxygen, and especially its by-products superoxide and peroxide, are dangerous to living tissue, and most anaerobic species must have been wiped out when it began to accumulate. Those which survived the change to aerobic life developed the enzymes catalase and peroxidase, with haem co-factors, to destroy peroxide, and an iron or manganese superoxide dismutase to convert superoxide ion to peroxide and oxygen.

Copper was predicted to be a latecomer in evolution, and we see it definitely appearing in the cytochrome oxidase of eucaryotes. Plastocyanin, an algal and plant cuproprotein associated most closely with system I of photosynthesis, does not appear in bacterial photosynthesis [23], though it is related to the bacterial respiratory protein azurin [59]. It is interesting, in the light of the endosymbiotic theory of the origin of the mitochondrion [42], that eucaryotic cytoplasm yields a superoxide dismutase containing copper and zinc, while mitochondria and bacteria yield the presumably more ancient proteins containing iron or manganese [10].

We can now suggest an evolutionary reason why iron plays so great and copper so small a part in photosynthesis and oxidative phosphorylation – copper remained chemically trapped in the ocean sediments until after these processes had developed. There is no trace of an early redox chemistry of manganese – we only see it appearing in photosynthesis as an oxygen-liberating factor, and later in superoxide dismutase. Presumably manganese could not, like iron or molybdenum, be adapted biologically to transfer electrons at low enough ambient redox potentials.

The reason why potassium and magnesium rather than sodium and calcium have become the essential intracellular bulk cations may be as follows. Early organisms, accumulating metabolites in their cytoplasm, had to correct the resulting osmotic imbalance by expelling some inessential solute, and among the cations, Na^+ was most abundant. Calcium also had to be expelled, as it would tend to bind to and precipitate the organic phosphates which were essential to the cell. Later in evolution it was to realize a great potential in its skeletal and trigger roles in animals (Chapter 2).

2 The non-redox roles of metals ions

This chapter is concerned mainly with the biochemistry of Na, K, Mg, Ca, Zn and Mn [72, 73]. Since we deal elsewhere with the areas of redox catalysis, metal metabolism and the bulk roles of metals, we are left with the rather diffuse regions of structural and non-redox catalytic roles. Metals can stabilize macromolecular structure, participate in cross-linking, affect the binding of small molecules and catalyse their reactions. They may induce conformation changes in enzymes, or in other proteins which may themselves enhance or inhibit enzyme activity. In many cases the details of how a metal exerts its influence on a catalysed reaction are not known, and the empirical distinction between metalloenzymes and metal-activated enzymes (according to whether pK_D for metal binding is greater or less than 7–8) is of no help in this question. We shall use the term 'catalytic' to indicate a

Table 2.1 Metal binding sites from X-ray structures

Protein	Metal	Ligands		Geometry
Carbonic anhydrase C	*Zn*	3HIS,H_2O		distorted tetr.
Carboxypeptidase A	*Zn*	2HIS,GLU,H_2O		distorted tetr.
Concanavalin A	Mn	GLU,HIS,$2H_2O$ ⎫		octahedral
		⎬ 2ASP		
(Mn–Ca = 530 pm)	Ca	TYR*,ASN,$2H_2O$ ⎭		octahedral
Erythrocuprein[†][‡]	Zn	2HIS,ASP ⎫		tetrahedral
		⎬ HIS		
(Zn–Cu = 600 pm)	*Cu*	3HIS ⎭		square planar
2–Zn insulin	Zn	3HIS, $3H_2O$		octahedral
4–Zn insulin	Zn–1	3HIS,$3H_2O$		octahedral
	Zn–2	2HIS,$2H_2O$		tetrahedral
Liver alcohol dehydrogenase	*Zn*–1	2HIS,CYS,H_2O		distorted tetr.
	Zn–2	4CYS		tetrahedral
Parvalbumin[‡]	Ca–CD	2ASP,2GLU,SER,PHE*		octahedral
	Ca–EF	3ASP,GLU,LYS*,H_2O		octahedral
Staphylococcal nuclease	*Ca*	THR,GLU,3ASP,H_2O		octahedral
Thermolysin	*Zn*	2HIS,GLU,H_2O		distorted tetr.
(Ca–Ca = 380 pm)	Ca–1	ASP,GLU*,H_2O ⎫		distorted oct.
		⎬ ASP,2GLU		
	Ca–2	ASN*, $2H_2O$ ⎭		distorted oct.
	Ca–3	2ASP,GLN*,$3H_2O$		distorted oct.
	Ca–4	TYR*,THR,THR*,ILE*,$2H_2O$		distorted oct.

Notes: Catalytic metals are italicized. *Ligation through main chain peptide carbonyl oxygen. [†]Cu is a *redox* site. [‡]See Fig. 2.1.

14

Fig. 2.1 Metal binding sites from X-ray structures (redrawn from [37] and [57]).
(a) The homologous C-D and E-F regions of parvalbumin. Ca^{2+} ions are octahedrally co-ordinated by ASP (51,53,90,92,94), GLU (59,62,101), SER (55), PHE*(57) and LYS*(96) residues (see note, Table 2.1).
(b) The active site in erythrocuprein. Cu^{2+} and Zn^{2+} are co-ordinated by HIS (44,46,61,69,78,118) and ASP (81). HIS (61) is not in a satisfactory position to ligate both metals at the same time.

site where a metal ion interacts directly with a reacting enzyme substrate, and 'structural' for all other binding, whether to other molecules or enzyme.

Structural information on metal binding sites comes both from crystallographic and solution studies. X-ray investigations on non-redox metals (Table 2.1, Fig. 2.1) are largely limited to calcium and zinc. One cannot often demonstrate that crystalline enzymes are in an active conformation, but this does not apply to enzymes studied in solution. Magnetic resonance [35] and optical spectra can yield data relating to the structural (and kinetic) properties of active species. NMR (nuclear magnetic resonance), in particular, can give detailed simultaneous information on a number of atoms of one type. The use of extrinsic probes (i.e. paramagnetic substituents which interact magnetically with the nuclei being observed) allows three-dimensional structures in solution to be inferred.

Since the non-redox metals generally do not have useful spectroscopic properties, much research on enzyme mechanisms involves substituted probe metals at active sites which produce only partial or no enzyme activity. Cases of substitution of one metal by another also sometimes occur *in vivo*, with or without loss of activity. Accordingly, in the first half of this chapter we look at some factors involved in metal activity, specificity and selectivity, before describing individual metals. In the second half we consider metals as general agents of physiological control.

2.1 Active sites of the non-redox metals

2.1.1 Metal activity, specificity and selectivity
Various theories have been put forward to explain the very high efficiency of enzyme-catalysed as compared with non-enzymatic

15

reactions. We shall mention here two ideas that relate to metals in catalytic roles. The first is that metal enzymes contain a 'super-acid' in neutral solution. That is to say, the bound metal presents a centre of positive charge, available for Lewis-acid catalysis, in pH ranges where comparable proton catalysis is ineffective, and where the free metal ion might be precipitated as hydroxide. Such a metal can interact with substrate molecules by polarizing bonds, neutralizing negative charge, spatially disposing ligands, and stabilizing transition states or intermediates.

The second idea, stemming from the unexpected spectroscopic properties of transition metals in many biological sites, is that metals may be bound in co-ordination geometries distorted for the sake of catalytic efficiency. The 'entatic' (strained) state of such metals [67] is produced by an arrangement of ligands different from the natural co-ordination assumed with small molecules in solution. Table 2.1 shows that in catalytic sites Zn is not allowed its normal regular tetrahedral co-ordination, although the importance of this in modifying its properties is difficult to assess. In fact, entatic states are particularly associated with redox enzymes and carriers, and probably not as a rule with non-redox sites. Phosphoglucomutase, for instance, seems to require metals in unstrained octahedral co-ordination for activation, as do many enzymes involved in ammonia and amine metabolism [16].

Against this background, what factors will affect the *specificity* of an active site, that is, the extent to which a metal ion cannot be substituted for without loss of activity? Size is important (Table 2.2). Ca^{2+}, the largest divalent cation, is *par excellence* the metal that cross-links macromolecules or induces large conformation changes in them. Bound to proteins, Ca^{2+} is usually six-co-ordinate, and can bind up to six different protein functional groups at the same time (Table 2.1). Mg^{2+}, on the other hand, although it can cross-link enzyme and substrate, tends to retain most of its tight hexaquo-co-ordination. Not surprisingly, since the two metals both prefer O-ligands, they often compete for binding, and may inhibit activity, at each other's sites. The same sort of competition occurs between Na^+ and K^+. With small ligands Ca^{2+} and K^+ are usually octa-co-ordinate, while Mg^{2+} and Na^+ are hexa-co-ordinate.

Many active sites are inactivated by a change of metal radius of

Table 2.2 Cationic radii in pm ($1\text{Å} = 100$ pm)

Li^+	74	Mg^{2+}	72	Mn^{2+}	82	Ni^{2+}	70
Na^+	102	Ca^{2+}	100	Fe^{2+}	77*	Cu^{2+}	73
K^+	138			Fe^{2+}	61[†]	Zn^{2+}	75
Rb^+	149			Co^{2+}	74	Cd^{2+}	95
Tl^+	150						
NH_4^+	145						

Notes: *High-spin state, [†]Low-spin state.

16

20 pm or less, with a wider tolerance when metal binds only to substrate, or has a purely structural role. (The high relative $[Na^+]_i$ of halophiles (Table 1.2) has led to the development of enzymes which are activated by both Na^+ and K^+.) In general we find that Rb^+, Tl^+, and NH_4^+ can often effectively substitute for K^+, and Mn^{2+} sometimes for Mg^{2+} However, the fact that the minor metals normally cannot substitute for Mg^{2+} or Ca^{2+} emphasizes that other factors are also involved in specificity.

For instance, the relative kinetic inertness of Ni^{2+} to ligand substitution probably explains why it is not such a good substitute for Mg^{2+} as is Mn^{2+}, even though it is closer in size. Nevertheless, it is more successful in activating phosphoglucomutase (PGM) than Mn^{2+}. In this case the catalytic role proposed is an unusual one for Mg^{2+} (see Fig. 2.2, p. 20). PGM also provides an example of the importance of stereochemical preferences in metal ions. While the optical spectrum of the active Ni-PGM indicates a regular octahedral co-ordination site, that of the inactive Co-PGM shows distortion of the site. The role of metal is thought to involve a regular hexa-co-ordination, as is natural for Mg^{2+} and Ni^{2+}.

Co and Zn provide one of the best examples of effective substitution. The two divalent ions are close both in size and in preferred ligand type and co-ordination geometry. As a result, Co^{2+} has been used widely as a spectroscopic probe in Zn-enzymes. The relative activity of Co^{2+} and Zn^{2+} in two Zn-enzymes is compared in Table 2.3 with that of other substituted ions. Co and Zn are comparable in activity for various reactions catalysed by both enzymes.

Binding site *selectivity*, i.e. relative affinity for different metals, is not to be confused with specificity of activation. In metabolic or structural sites, which only require a given metal to be bound strongly, selectivity and specificity usually go together. In catalytic sites, however, there is no necessary relation between the two. (This is illustrated well by the data in Table 2.3.)

Table 2.3 Substituted Zn-enzymes: metal activities and affinities

| M^{2+} | Human carbonic anhydrase B | | | Carboxypeptidase A | | |
	Anhydrase*	Esterase†	pK_D	Peptidase‡	Esterase§	pK_D
Mn	4.3	14	3.8	8	35	4.6
Co	66	324	7.2	160	95	7.0
Ni	7	12.2	9.5	106	87	8.2
Cu	1.3	18.6	11.6	0	0	10.6
Zn	100	100	10.5	100	100	10.5
Cd	4.7	7.3	9.2	0	150	10.8
Hg	0.07	3.2	21.5	0	116	21.0

Notes: Activities (k_{cat}) relative to Zn = 100 in each case for the reactions * $CO_2 + OH^- \rightleftharpoons HCO_3^-$, †$p$-nitrophenyl acetate hydrolysis, ‡carbobenzoxyglycyl-L-phenylalanine hydrolysis, §hippuryl-dl-β-phenyl-lactate hydrolysis. Data recalculated from [17].

Selectivity is achieved [61] by providing a co-ordination site suited to a particular metal's charge, ionic radius, preferred geometry (e.g. tetrahedral for Zn^{2+}, square planar for Cu^{2+}, octahedral for Mg^{2+}), and chemical type ('hard' ligands such as O-functions for metals of groups IA and IIA, 'soft' ligands such as N and S atoms for transition metals, especially in lower valence states.) However, biological selectivity involves more than just binding affinities. This is particularly true of entatic sites, where distortions of geometry may relatively destabilize the binding of the active metal. Metabolic factors are also important, for instance metal availability, buffering of competing metals, and the specific action of chelatase enzymes (Chapter 5).

2.1.2 The alkali metals

Over fifty enzymes are known to be activated by alkali metals [13]. Most, being intracellular, are activated by K^+ and inhibited by Na^+. It is thought that the alkali metals generally have structural roles. In some cases protein subunits combine to give active oligomers under the influence of M^+ (adenosine deaminase, N^{10}-formyltetrahydrofolate synthetase), while in others conformational changes are induced (pyruvate kinase, yeast L-homoserine dehydrogenase), which may affect the binding of substrates or inhibitors (phosphofructokinase). Monovalent cations are involved in the binding of coenzyme B_{12} to some of its apoenzymes, and in the activation of further regulatory enzymes including yeast pyruvate carboxylase and the δ-aminolaevulinic acid dehydrase of Rhodospirillum spheroides.

The best described example of a K-activated enzyme is pyruvate kinase (PK), which also requires Mg. It exists in temperature-dependent forms, the high-temperature (active) form being stabilized by the binding of Mg^{2+} which, in turn, is promoted by K^+. The tetrameric enzyme (mol wt 237000) binds four molecules each of K^+, Mg^{2+} and substrate phosphoenolpyruvate (PEP). By using the NMR probes $^{205}Tl^+$ or $CH_3NH_3^+$ (for K^+), and Mn^{2+} as a spin label (for Mg^{2+}), the distance between the two metals has been estimated in a catalytically active system [43]. It is found to be 820 pm in the complex PK/M^+/M^{2+}. This decreases to 490 pm upon binding of PEP, apparently as a result of a substrate-induced conformation change. K^+ is, therefore, bound near the active site, though its role is unknown. The use of NMR spectroscopy opens up a field of study on these enzymes, where the role of the electronically 'silent' alkali metals is as yet little understood.

The halobacteria and halococci [38] are micro-organisms which not only tolerate, but actively require a very concentrated NaCl medium for growth. They thrive, for instance, in media of 4 M NaCl + 320 mM K^+. As intracellular ionic strength matches that outside (Table 1.2), an osmotic problem is avoided, at the expense of developing salt-stable intracellular structures and mechanisms.

At least twenty enzymes from extreme halopholic bacteria have been studied, and found to have a high, even maximal, activities in high alkali salt concentration, and to be denatured in low-salt conditions. Ribosomes are similarly affected (while those of non-halophiles break down in alkali chloride over 150 mM), and the rod-shaped halobacterium cell envelope is only maintained in 4 M NaCl.

Alkali metal roles associated with membrane transport are described in Chapter 5. Apart from the important activation of membrane ATPase (the alkali ion pump), Na^+ concentration gradients may be used to drive the transport of other molecules across cell membranes, for instance sugars and amino-acids inwards, and Ca^{2+} outwards.

2.1.3 Magnesium

The essential nature of Mg^{2+} and K^+ for all forms of life is seen in their interactions with nucleic acids: in stabilizing ribosome and nucleic acid structure, and in activating enzymes concerned with synthesizing RNA, DNA and proteins. Mn^{2+} can substitute for Mg^{2+} in many of these situations, but usually leads to inaccuracy. With Mn^{2+} and ribosomes, for instance, errors in translation occur, and DNA polymerase is enabled to incorporate ribonucleotides as well as deoxy-ribonucleotides. Mg^{2+} is involved in the assembly of microtubules, and (like Ca^{2+} outside the cell) is thought to bind to anionic sites on the plasma membrane. In view of its affinity for phosphate groups, it is no surprise to find that the ion is usually involved in the reactions of ATP and ADP.

Most of the enzymatic roles of Mg^{2+} can be described as catalysing the transfer of phosphate or phosphocompounds. Nucleophilic substitution at phosphorus may be of type S_N1 (with a planar PO_3 intermediate) or S_N2 (with a five-co-ordinate intermediate $X-PO_3-Y$). The effect of binding proton, metal or alkyl to the central (transferred) PO_3 is to favour the second mechanism, and most of the mechanistic proposals for enzymatic phosphoryl and nucleotidyl transfer are of this type. Evidence has been obtained by the substitution of spectroscopic probes like Mn^{2+} and Co^{2+} for Mg^{2+}. NMR and ESR have been used extensively to determine distances between divalent (and monovalent) cations, P, F, C and H atoms, as well as kinetic and other parameters in inactive and active complexes. The general role of Mn^{2+} (and presumably Mg^{2+}) is to bind the PO_3 being transferred.

A broad distinction, originally made on the basis of proton relaxation enhancement (an NMR technique) with Mn^{2+}, is between enzymes in which M^{2+} is bound only to substrate, and those in which it is bound to the enzyme surface as well. The former group have less exacting metal requirements, and may even be activated by Ca^{2+}. A different role, that of promoting the ionization of an active site SER, has been proposed for Mg^{2+} in phosphoglucomutase, though the evidence is not compelling [43]. Here the metal also provides a pivot for the rotation of the glucose molecule. Fig. 2.2 shows this and other

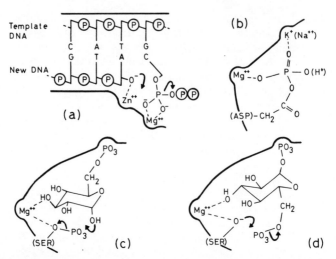

Fig. 2.2 Phosphoryl transfer enzymes: some proposed active sites, based mainly on magnetic resonance data. (Protons on phosphate groups have been ignored except in (b) where protonation is thought to coincide with Na^+-binding.) (a) *DNA polymerase*. Zn^{2+} shown activating ribose 3′-hydroxyl for nucleophilic attack on the α-phosphate of new CTP, which is bound by Mg^{2+}. (b) *Na/K ATPase* (kidney microsome). Mg^{2+} binds the phosphoryl group being transferred from ATP to the free carboxylate of ASP. Phosphorylation and phosphate release are both cytoplasmic, in the presence of bound Na^+ and K^+ respectively. (c) *Phosphoglucomutase*. 1-phosphorylation of glucose-6-phosphate by phosphoserine. Mg^{2+} stabilizes leaving group. (d) 6-dephosphorylation of glucose-1,6-diphosphate. Mg^{2+}-3-OH bond provides a pivot for the rotation of glucose.

active site complexes proposed for various phosphoryl transfer enzymes.

Another important and unique role of Mg is its appearance in chlorophyll. Arrays of chlorophyll molecules in photosynthetic bacteria or plant chloroplasts serve to trap radiant energy to drive the chemical reduction of CO_2 in photosynthesis. Any of the molecules can absorb an energy quantum of appropriate wavelength, which can migrate rapidly between them until it reaches a reaction centre (possibly involving a modified chlorophyll). Here it generates separated oxidizing and reducing chemical species (p. 43).

Mg^{2+} lies in the centre of the chlorin ring (Fig. 3.1), slightly out of plane. The X-ray structure of a bacteriochlorophyll protein [20] seems to indicate that Mg^{2+}, together with the phytyl side-chain, is used to tether individual molecules to protein side-chains on the inside of a hollow shell. However, this is an unusual situation, and chlorophyll is thought usually to be active as pairs of molecules in a lipid environment.

2.1.4 Calcium

Many Ca-proteins [37] are found outside the cell. Most are digestive enzymes with K_D for Ca^{2+} of the order 0.1–1 mM, appropriate to the metal concentration in animal plasma. (α-amylase is exceptional with $K_D \sim 1\,\mu M$.) Since Ca^{2+} is required for activity, these enzymes are 'switched on' as they come into contact with the ion, ensuring that they only become active after they have left the cytoplasm. The role of Ca^{2+} is usually structural (in our sense), with the possible exception of a catalytic function in staphylococcal nuclease. Ca^{2+} binds to trypsinogen, labilizing it for proteolytic conversion to trypsin, and thereafter stabilizes it against further attack by binding at a second site on the molecule. It is commonly found that Ca-binding stabilizes proteins against proteolysis, and sometimes against heat as well (e.g. thermolysin).

The conversion of fibrinogen to fibrin in blood clotting is the result of a remarkable cascade of sequential proteolytic reactions Several of the factors involved are proproteases, activated and then stabilized (like trypsin) in the presence of Ca^{2+}. Of these, the homologous factors II (prothrombin), VII, IX and X contain γ-carboxy-glutamate residues, which are formed in a post-transcriptional modification requiring Vitamin K, and bind Ca^{2+} weakly. Prothrombin, for instance, contains ten such residues, which possibly mediate its Ca-induced structural transition, and (cross-linked by Ca^{2+} to membrane phospholipids) its binding to cell surfaces. The thrombin-catalysed formation of fibrin is also accelerated by the action of Ca^{2+} through the activation of factor XIII, a cross-linking transglutaminase, and possibly through direct binding to fibrin. (The importance of citrating blood for transfusion, to bind Ca^{2+} and prevent coagulation, is obvious.) In invertebrates, a Ca-transaminase is important for haemostasis, and another protein of invertebrate fluids, haemocyanin, is also stabilized by Ca^{2+}.

External Ca^{2+} bound to the plasma membrane is probably very important in conditioning its kinetic and structural properties. This is not well understood at the biochemical level, but on p. 26, for instance, we describe some physiological effects of Ca^{2+} on Na^+-permeability in excitable tissue.

Intracellular Ca-triggered enzymes and proteins must bind Ca^{2+} in the presence of a 1000-fold excess of Mg^{2+}: accordingly they show high selectivity for Ca^{2+} with pK_D in the range 5–8. The structure of parvalbumin (Tables 2.1 and 2.4, Fig. 2.1), shows two high-affinity sites, each with a similar metal hexa-co-ordination at a helix–coil–helix junction in the protein chain. Each of these sites is homologous with Ca-binding sites in troponin-C, Vitamin D-induced Ca-binding protein (p. 63), the modulator protein of cyclic mononucleotide metabolism (p. 26), and with non-binding regions of myosin. Binding at all these high-affinity sites produces marked protein conformational changes.

The most familiar biological occurrence of calcium is in mineralized tissue. Calcified structures are most commonly found in animals, as phosphate (bone, dentin and dental enamel) or carbonate (eggshells, invertebrate skeletons). A few calcium oxalate structures are known, and examples of calcification are found in plants and bacteria. Calcium carbonate occurs in the mineral forms calcite, aragonite, or occasionally veratite, according to the physiology of deposition.

Bone is formed around collagen, which gives high tensile strength – the decalcification of a bone leaves a flexible collagenous matrix of the same shape. Human bone contains around 70% by weight of the mineral hydroxyapatite, $Ca_{10}(PO_4)_6(OH)_2$. Between one and two thirds of this is crystalline, according to maturity. 40 nm long needles of the salt attach to collagen fibres, interleaving and preventing slippage between them. Electron micrographs of embryonic bone show crystallites on collagen in close alignment with the cross-striations of the latter.

Although the deposition of mineral salts requires their solubility product to be exceeded in the surrounding fluid, this is not a sufficient condition, as calcium readily forms metastable supersaturated solutions with both carbonate and phosphate. The process involves nucleation of crystal growth at the right site, and subsequent prevention of poisoning of the extending crystal surface. *A priori*, we might expect that an array of organically bound oxyanions with suitable spacing, corresponding to a mineral crystal lattice, might constitute such a nucleation site. Various compounds have been proposed as forming nucleation centres, including chondroitin sulphate, phosphoproteins [65], and acidic phospholipids [49]. The first sign of mineralization in growth regions of epiphyseal cartilage and dentin is the appearance of vesicles in the extracellular matrix in which crystallites are seen attached to the inner surface of the lipid envelope. However, the relationship of these to phosphoproteins, phospholipids and collagen in calcification remains obscure.

Finally, bone is a vital tissue, continually being resorbed and remodelled throughout life, and able to act as a buffer for body Ca and phosphate. It is believed that metabolically active bone is bathed in a K-rich fluid within a cellular membrane, which separates it from circulating body fluids and, under hormonal influence, regulates the transfer of mineral salts.

2.1.5 Zinc and other metals

Zn plays a catalytic role in a number of metallo-enzymes [1, 3, 17]. We shall exemplify two possible 'superacid' mechanisms. In the first, weak O-ligands (for which Zn^{2+} would naturally have a low affinity) are presented directly to the metal so that a C–O bond is polarized prior to reaction. In the second, Zn^{2+} enhances the nucleophilicity of H_2O or hydroxy-groups by promoting their deprotonation. In both cases, binding of reagents to Zn^{2+} helps orient them for subsequent reaction. It was predicted from spectroscopic data on Co-substituted enzymes that Zn might be found to occupy distorted tetrahedral sites, and this has been confirmed in several cases (Table 2.1). These sites contrast with the more regular structural sites.

The Zn in carboxypeptidase lies in the wall of a shallow cleft which accommodates the peptide substrate. Here X-ray studies show clearly that, unless the binding geometry of substrate analogues is quite artificial, peptide carbonyl oxygen must enter the first co-ordination sphere of Zn^{2+}. It is proposed that Zn^{2+} polarizes the peptide bond prior to nucleophilic attack.

The activity of carbonic anhydrase [53] involves an acidic group with $pK_a \sim 7$. In a plausible mechanism of action, this group is identified as a water molecule co-ordinated to Zn^{2+}. Substrate CO_2 lies outside the first co-ordination sphere of Zn^{2+}, and is attacked by the co-ordinated hydroxyl ion to give HCO_3^-. The entatic nature of the Zn site is thought to be important in determining the pK_a of the co-ordinated water. The cell nucleus in particular accumulates Zn, and both RNA and DNA polymerases contain tightly bound ions, apparently interacting with the polynucleotide chains (Fig. 2.2).

There is not much structural knowledge of the natural non-redox sites of Mn. Mn^{2+} activates a number of hydrolases (e.g. arginase) and carboxylases (e.g. malic enzyme), as well as enzymes in phosphate metabolism (compare Mg^{2+}). Most dehydrogenases are not metal-dependent: the action of Mn^{2+} in isocitrate dehydrogenase may be to anchor the substrate in an α-enolcarboxy chelate:

$$\begin{array}{c} \text{HOOC-CH} \\ \text{HOOC} \end{array} \!\!\! C\!=\!C \!\!\! \begin{array}{c} \text{CO-O}^- \\ | \\ \text{O}\!-\!\text{Mn}^{2+}\!-\text{enzyme} \end{array}$$

The only high-affinity non-redox Mn-enzyme is pyruvate carboxylase, which is equally well activated by Mg^{2+}. The low affinity of most sites for Mn^{2+} presents a problem in determining its actual physiological roles. However, the effects of Mn deficiency on blood and connective tissue have indicated that various glycosyl transferases are activated by Mn *in vivo*.

A number of the other minor metals listed in Chapter 1 may have non-redox roles. Among them is Fe, which activates aconitase in the citric acid cycle. Aconitase isomerases citrate to isocitrate via aconitate, and an elegant mechanism of action, the 'ferrous wheel' has been proposed [25] on the basis of model Fe^{II} complexes. Another non-redox role for Fe may be in the activation of phospho-enolpyruvate carboxykinase [41].

2.2 Regulatory and trigger roles of metal ions
Usually one can consider the actions of metal enzymes against the background of a constant stoichiometry of bound metal, either because the active metal is very strongly bound, or because its free concentration is subject to homeostasis. However, there are some areas where variation in free metal ion concentration is used as a control mechanism. Elsewhere we refer to the 'switching on' of extracellular enzymes activated by Ca^{2+}, and to the influence of metals on processes concerned with their own metabolism. Here we shall go on to discuss two main

topics: the activation of regulatory enzymes, and the dramatic 'trigger' actions of Ca^{2+} as it enters various animal cells.

2.2.1 Metal ions and regulatory enzymes

It is not surprising that many regulatory enzymes, being intracellular, are activated by K^+ or Mg^{2+} and inhibited by Na^+ or Ca^{2+}. It does not necessarily follow that these metals play any part in the regulation of metabolism, especially in animal cells where their concentrations are closely controlled. For a regulatory role to be possible, an enzyme must become activated or inhibited within the natural range of concentration variation of the metal concerned. Many examples of competitive inhibition by metal ions, for instance of the glycolytic enzymes by Ca^{2+}, are probably not important when considered against actual free ion levels in the cell. We mention here three cases where Mg^{2+} may have regulatory importance, before considering Na and other metals. (Ca is described later.)

The potential of Mg^{2+} as a general regulator of animal cell metabolism is shown in experiments on cultured chick fibroblasts [58]. Mg^{2+} deprivation resulted in inhibition of growth, and affected the metabolism of proteins, carbohydrates, lipids and nucleic acids, as well as differentiated functions like collagen synthesis. The same effects were also produced by deprivation of Ca^{2+} or serum, and by changes in population density or pH, and moreover could be mimicked by adjusting free intracellular Mg^{2+} with chelate buffers such as pyrophosphate ion. It was therefore suggested that all the external influences were mediated by a reduction in free intracellular Mg^{2+}. This might be achieved by means of a variable capacity Mg store, possibly involving binding to phospholipids or other groups on the inner surface of the cell membrane.

Insulin stimulates glycogen formation, glycolysis and protein synthesis in muscle, and many enzymes in these processes are either allosterically activated by Mg^{2+}, or utilize Mg^{2+}-ATP as a substrate. In one case, it has been shown that enzyme Mg-binding and activity both changed under the influence of insulin [50]. Total phosphoglucomutase (PGM) protein in rabbit muscle was found not to vary with fasting or insulin administration. However, enzymatic activity increased more than two-fold when fasted animals were administered insulin. It was found that some of the PGM was effectively inactivated by the competitive substitution of Zn^{2+} for Mg^{2+}, and that the effect of insulin was to increase the proportion of the active Mg–PGM from 35% to 83% of the (constant) total. This change may have been due to an increase in free cytoplasmic Mg^{2+}, possibly even released from the inner cell membrane surface, since insulin is known to affect membrane permeability and affinity for solutes.

When a metal–ATP complex is the true substrate of an enzyme, then inhibition by metal-free ATP may occur, so that catalytic efficiency depends on the ratio of divalent metal to ATP. Sometimes the free metal ion itself may inhibit the enzyme, so that an excess of free M^{2+} *or* free ATP over the other will reduce enzyme activity. This is the case with hexokinase [54], which regulates glucose metabolism in erythrocytes. Within the erythrocyte, deoxyhaemoglobin is capable of binding 85% of diphosphoglycerate and 35% of ATP, and on saturation with oxygen it releases these small organic phosphates, which can then bind Mg^{2+}. The resultant calculated change of free $[Mg^{2+}]_i$, from 1.9 mM to 0.57 mM, might well be sufficient to reduce hexokinase activity in oxygen-loaded erythrocytes.

The bacterium *Klebsiella pneumoniae* (*Aerobacter aerogenes*) shows an intriguing *Na requirement* [48]. Under aerobic conditions, it metabolizes Na^+ or K^+ citrate via the citric acid cycle. Anaerobically it requires Na^+ for the fermentation of citrate, leading to excretion of acetate. The enzymes citrate lyase and a Na-activated oxaloacetate decarboxylase appear, and energy is presumably derived from the metabolism of pyruvate by means such as the phosphoroclastic reaction. Under conditions of aeration (reduced O_2), only in the presence of Na^+ are the two fermentative enzymes induced, and α-oxoglutarate dehydrogenase of the citric acid cycle repressed. We may surmise that one of the effects of O_2 limitation on this organism is to starve the membrane ion pumps of ATP, allowing K^+ efflux and Na^+ influx, and that the latter possibly helps to mediate the change to anaerobic metabolism.

Metals also play an intriguing role in the control of secondary metabolism [70]. (This is defined as the elaboration of specialized compounds or structures with no growth function, by micro-organisms which have stopped dividing.) Micro-organisms commonly require minor metals in ambient concentrations of $0.1 \, \mu M$ for growth, and will tolerate them up to 1 mM. However, the course of secondary metabolism is critically affected by concentration variation between these limits. Toxin production by the diphtheria bacillus, for instance, only occurs in a narrow range of Fe concentrations. Below $1 \, \mu M$, cell activity is depressed, while above $10 \, \mu M$ toxin synthesis is inhibited. As well as many species-specific effects, Mn has wide-ranging effects on bacilli, Fe on other bacteria, and Zn on fungi. The effect of Mn on bacilli is expressed in raised levels of Mn-activated enzymes prior to secondary metabolite production or endospore formation. Many secondary metabolites are ionophores and/or antibiotics, but no unitary theory of the significance or specificity of metals in their production has emerged.

2.2.2 *The trigger roles of calcium*
Cytoplasmic Ca^{2+} is usually maintained at levels below $1 \, \mu M$ in animal tissue. An influx of Ca^{2+} producing an increase of $[Ca^{2+}]_i$ from $0.1-10 \, \mu M$ is found to stimulate a number of vital processes. These actions, in response to external stimulation of the cell by various means, constitute the trigger roles of Ca^{2+}. (Two special examples,

control of secretion and of muscle contraction, are described in following sections.)

One mode of entry of Ca^{2+} into the cytoplasm is the process of membrane depolarization [56]. Typically, Na^+/K^+ depolarization of excitable membranes in nerve or muscle is initiated externally by an altered ionic environment or by the binding of a neurotransmitter. Physiological Na^+ channels open, allowing an influx of Na^+ and a local depolarization. (This is antagonized by high $[Ca^{2+}]_e$, which is thought to play a role in keeping the Na^+ channels closed.) If the local effect is sufficient, a depolarization wave is propagated along the membrane, as the channels also open in response to a drop in transmembrane potential. Similar voltage-dependent channels, distinct from the rapid Na^+-channels, mediate an influx of Ca^{2+}, and in some tissues, Ca^{2+} rather than Na^+ plays a major role in depolarization. Na^+ influx is followed by an efflux of K^+ (through channels that close more slowly) so that repolarization occurs, and the concentration imbalance is eventually restored by the membrane ion pumps.

The binding of hormones to their target cells may also result in Ca^{2+} influx. Here the immediate actions of Ca^{2+} are closely related to those of the cyclic nucleotides cAMP and cGMP, which are effective over a similar low concentration range. The cyclic nucleotides are formed from ATP and GTP by cyclase enzymes in the cell membrane orientated towards the cytoplasm, and they are inactivated by a phosphodiesterase. Ca^{2+}, cAMP and cGMP are in fact inter-related 'second messengers', mediating the effects of various hormones on cells. They influence each other by a few key control interactions, including the following [55]. First, Ca^{2+} acts as a coupling factor in hormonal stimulation of adenyl cyclase, but when $[Ca^{2+}]_i$ rises, it inhibits the enzyme. Second, it may activate or inhibit phosphodiesterase. Third, cAMP itself can affect Ca^{2+} flux across membranes. In particular, it is thought to be able to promote Ca^{2+} efflux from mitochondria, uptake by microsomes and sarcoplasmic reticulum, and influx across the cell membrane. All these effects can be elaborated diversely for the requirements of different tissues.

The stimulation of adenylate cyclase and phosphodiesterase is effected by a 'modulator protein' which undergoes a large conformational change on binding Ca^{2+}. This protein, found in all animal cells, resembles troponin-C (see p. 21) and can activate myofibril *in vitro*. It may be involved in smooth muscle contraction, and also in erythrocyte membrane Ca-transport.

Although the rise in $[Ca^{2+}]_i$ in response to nervous or chemical stimulation of the cell may trigger secretion or muscular contraction (see below), it may also have an effect on metabolism. Ca^{2+} affects glycogenolysis both by its influence on cAMP, which activates protein kinase, and by direct activation of phosphorylase b kinase. It also activates tyrosine hydroxylase (p. 56) *in vitro*, and is thought in part to mediate the stimulation of this enzyme in nerve by action potentials [45]. Several key mitochondrial enzymes are activated by Ca^{2+} at μ-molar concentrations, including α-glycerophosphate dehydrogenase and succinate dehydrogenase on the inner membrane, and pyruvate dehydrogenase phosphate phosphatase. It is known that mitochondrial uptake of ADP for oxidative phosphorylation cannot compete with uptake of Ca^{2+} at the same concentration as ADP. This raises the possibility that Ca^{2+} may in some way be involved in control of oxidative phosphorylation and the citric acid cycle.

2.2.3 Secretion from cytoplasmic granules
Some generalizations can be made about the discharge of the contents of 'export' vesicles from cells, whether stimulated by nerve impulse or chemical messenger. All such processes depend on extra-cellular Ca^{2+}, and most have been shown to involve exocytosis. However, the means by which Ca^{2+} acts in the cell are controversial [62].

In a group of cell types which include adrenal chromaffin cells, neurones, neurosecretory fibres and pancreatic β-cells, Ca^{2+} influx directly causes exocytosis. Ca^{2+} entry is promoted by the actions of the appropriate chemical messenger (e.g. acetyl choline, glucose), or by membrane depolarization. The latter is dependent on extracellular Na^+ and K^+, but while increased $[Na^+]_e$ stimulates depolarization, it depresses secretion. The effect of increased $[K^+]_e$ is to mimic the action of the secretogogue, while external Mg^{2+} is inhibitory. It is probable that Ca^{2+} and Na^+ enter through voltage-dependent channels.

Another group of cells, notably mast cells, together with some salivary and pancreatic cells, differ from this pattern in their response to K^+. Decrease in membrane potential may be experienced without a resulting Ca^{2+} influx, which seems in mast cells to depend on a specific hypersensitivity reaction on the cell surface. There is also evidence that these cells, on stimulation, release Ca^{2+} into the cytoplasm from intracellular stores.

2.2.4 Activation of muscle contraction
Muscular contraction depends for its energy on the Mg-activated hydrolysis of ATP by the protein myosin, and is triggered by an in-

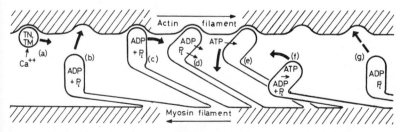

Fig. 2.3 Proposed mechanism of myofibrial contraction (see text).

27

crease in $[Ca^{2+}]_i$. The muscle proteins actin and myosin each form polymeric filaments, which lie parallel to each other within the myofibril. It is thought the array of actin filaments is pulled along relative to the array of myosin filaments by a ratchet mechanism (Fig. 2.3). Actin and myosin are reversibly cross-linked by the flexible protruding heads of the myosin subunits. In the contraction sequence, binding of myosin to actin via these heads (b) triggers the power stroke, a flexing of the heads (c), and ADP and inorganic phosphate (P_i) are released (d). The binding of fresh ATP to myosin then allows the actomyosin complex to dissociate (e), and hydrolysis of ATP on myosin leads to a return stroke in which the myosin head extends (f), with storage of conformational energy for the next stroke (g), (b).

In resting muscle, this cycle is inhibited at the first step: the trigger action of Ca^{2+} is to release the inhibition. The myosin-binding sites on the actin filament are blocked by the proteins troponin (TN) and tropomyosin (TM). Ca^{2+} binds strongly to TN, which in turn causes TM to move off the sites (a), allowing myosin to bind. The mechanism shows how while lack of Ca^{2+} in the presence of ATP relaxes muscle (actomyosin dissociated), lack of ATP (for instance after prolonged stimulation) results in rigor, since actomyosin cannot dissociate, stage (e).

Three components of troponin have been identified, and are designated according to their principle interactions (Table 2.4). TN-I can itself inhibit actomyosin formation, TN-T is essential for interaction with tropomyosin, and TN-C binds Ca^{2+} strongly. The reversible binding of Ca^{2+} to TN-C produces marked conformational changes in the protein, and promotes strong binding of TN-C to TN-I with the removal of the latter from its inhibitory site. The relation between TN-I and the action of tropomyosin is not known, but there is evidence that tropomyosin extends the inhibitory effect of TN-I to actin

Table 2.4 Some Ca-binding proteins in muscle

Protein	Mol wt	Ca sites	pK_D
Myofibril			
Troponin (TN)	80 000		
= TN–C	17 500	2	6–7
		2	8–9
+ TN–I	23 000	–	
+ TN–T	37 000	–	
Sarcoplasm			
Phosphorylase *b* kinase	1.3×10^6	24	6–7
Parvalbumin (fish)	11 000	2	6–7
Sarcoplasmic reticulum			
Calsequestrin	44 000	43	3–4
High affinity protein	55 000	1	5–6
		25	4
Exterior acid component	20 – 30 000	ca. 3	6
Ca/Mg ATPase	100 000	2	6–7

subunits with which the latter is not directly in contact. (In molluscs which lack troponin, Ca^{2+} apparently acts by binding to part of the myosin molecule, with the same result of actomyosin formation.)

Because of the high cellular concentration of actomyosin (ca. 0.1 mM), and for speed of activation, muscle cells cannot rely only on the influx of Ca^{2+} from the cell membrane to stimulate contraction. According to muscle type, extra Ca^{2+} is stored either in the sarcoplasmic reticulum (white muscle) or in mitochondria (heart, and perhaps red and smooth muscle). Release of Ca^{2+} from the Ca-binding proteins of the former is probably triggered directly by the electrical depolarization of the cell membrane. Release from mitochondria may be triggered by chemical messengers such as Na^+ or cAMP [55]. By means of these internal stores, $[Ca^{2+}]_i$ can rise from 0.1 μM (myofibrils relaxed) to 10 μM (troponin fully activated) in a few milliseconds, with myosin ATPase activity increasing 100-fold.

3 Electron transfer and redox reactions

Redox (oxidation–reduction) reactions occur everywhere in biochemistry. The transfer of a hydride ion to or from carbon is a fundamental redox reaction, usually mediated by a flavin or pyridinium nucleotide (both organic co-factors). However, there are areas of redox biochemistry where metals (Fe, Cu, Mo, Mn, Co) have an essential role, most notably in electron transfer and the handling of certain small inorganic species [8].

With metal co-factors, we can distinguish groups solely involved in *electron transfer* from those involved in *substrate redox reactions*. The former are protected from solvent by their protein environment, and electrons are passed to or from the active metal via the protein in some way. The latter, on the other hand, are 'open-sided' groups, and allow co-ordination or close approach of substrate molecules as well as electron transfer if required.

In this chapter we shall look at some of the general properties that suit metals for these roles, and at some of the well characterized electron transfer chromophores (haem, 'blue' copper, and iron–sulphur clusters) as they occur in simple and complex proteins. Then follow sections on Mo and Co (coenzyme B_{12}) enzymes, and finally a survey of the components of the electron transfer chains of respiration and photosynthesis. In the next chapter we shall describe one particular group of proteins with open-sided metal co-factors – those which react with dioxygen species.

3.1 Metals as redox catalysts

Transition metals, with their labile d-electron systems, are well suited to catalyse redox reactions, for the following reasons. (1) A range of accessible oxidation states enables them to transfer electrons. (2) The redox potentials (E_o') for such transfer can be varied by alteration of ligand type or geometry. (3) Metals mediate atom transfer reactions. (4) Stable paramagnetic states are common, facilitating reaction with radical substrates. (5) The degree of paramagnetism (spin-state) can be varied. (6) Metals can bind neutral as well as anionic ligands. The last four points apply especially to open-sided sites.

Most organic redox co-factors, including the ubiquitous hydride carriers NAD(P)H, deal in the transfer of pairs of electrons ($H^- \equiv H^+ + 2e^-$), thus avoiding unstable or readily autoxidizable intermediates. However, all the metal chromophores referred to above have working capacities *in vivo* of only one electron, with no atom transfer. (It is the alternation of these two types of redox carrier which permits the translocation of protons, p. 44.) Open-sided sites have greater capacities for change in oxidation state, as atom transfer or ion-binding nearby can offset local charge changes induced by electron transfer. Haem Fe, for instance, can vary from $+2$ to $+5$ in various reactions, and Mn and Mo are capable of similar changes *in vitro* at least.

The range of redox potentials at which metal co-factors are reported to operate is very wide, from -300 to ca. $+800\,mV$ (haem in cyt P450 and cyt a_3), from $+180$ to $+767\,mV$ (blue Cu in plastocyanin and fungal laccase), and from -490 to $+350\,mV$ (iron–sulphur in ferredoxin and HiPIP). E_o' for a group may even be varied during the course of a reaction, with the effect of controlling electron flow. Organic groups rarely reach the oxidizing extremes of metals (perhaps in photosynthesis?), but flavodoxin substitutes functionally for ferredoxin in Fe-deficient *Clostridium pasteurianum*, with flavin E_o' values of -170 and $-380\,mV$ for two-step reduction.

Co in coenzyme B_{12} enzymes is probably the only metal catalysing C-atom transfer reactions. However, metals have an important role in O-atom ('oxene') transfer. This occurs in the splitting of peroxide, and probably in oxygenation and in the reduction of the oxyanions of N and S. The first step in the reactions of the peroxidases, for instance, is probably (see p. 58) of the form

$$Fe^{III}\text{-}\bar{O}\text{-}OH \longrightarrow Fe^{V}O^{2-}(cpd\ I) + OH^{-}$$

Here transfer of oxene from peroxide to Fe^{III} in haem raises the formal Fe oxidation state from $+3$ to $+5$, though the charge on oxide (-2) and porphyrin (-2) serve to keep the net charge at $+1$. (The formation of oxycations such as $Fe^{IV}O^{2-}$ is a feature of the chemistry of Fe, Mn and Mo, though not particularly of Cu. Nevertheless, Cu catalysis is responsible for splitting the O–O bond in laccase.) By means of such atom transfer, and by the assembly of groups of redox chromophores, metalloproteins can act as electron converters in redox transfer chains. Cytochrome oxidase converts the four oxidizing equivalents of O_2 rapidly into single units carried by cyt c, and nitrogenase enables six electrons to react with N_2 to yield ammonia. (In a similar way, flavin can act as a two-to-one converter by hydride and electron transfer.)

Paramagnetic states of metals are commonly used in initial activation of the stable diradical O_2, although O_2 reacts satisfactorily with haemocyanin, which is diamagnetic in its cuprous form. The spin state of a metal reflects the degree to which its electrons are paired with each other. From our point of view, one important aspect of electron pairing is that it affects the interaction of a metal with its ligands. Fe in haem, for instance, may adopt an octahedral co-ordination, lying in the haem plane, with two axial ligands. This induces a low-spin state, in which Fe^{II} is diamagnetic. In the high-spin state, ligand bonds are weakened and lengthened, and Fe shifts slightly out of the haem plane to become five-co-ordinate. This movement in part mediates a mutual influence of protein conformation and Fe state on each other. When protein influence maintains open-sided haem in a low-spin state, a substrate molecule in an axial co-ordination position is bound more strongly, and is kinetically less likely to be released, than from a high-spin haem Fe. This is one mechanism which helps to prevent the loss of active intermediates from catalytic sites.

When two paramagnetic atoms are close to each other, their magnetic moments interact and tend to align in contrary directions. This 'spin-coupling' leads to a net loss of paramagnetism, so that a substance containing pairs of identical atoms with completely coupled spins would in fact be diamagnetic. The EPR signals of spin-coupled atoms are broadened, sometimes to undetectability (e.g. in laccase). It is this type of magnetic evidence, confirmed in some cases by X-ray results (e.g. in haemerythrin), that we shall refer to often in this chapter and the next as evidence of metal proximity. The designations Fe_2 and Cu_2 used in Chapter 4 indicate no more than open-sided sites with pairs of magnetically interacting metal atoms closer than 600 pm.

The binding of neutral molecules to metals is well demonstrated in the carrier–O_2 complexes, and a Mo–N_2 interaction is probably essential for nitrogenase activity. The type of complex formed can vary from the non-ionic (e.g. oxymyoglobin) to the ionic (oxy-complexes of haemocyanin and haemerythrin.) The latter may depend for their success on the binding of reversibly reduced O_2 (i.e. peroxide) between two positive centres in the metal pair groups. Such ligations of nucleophilic groups is also vital in binding active metals, and ligation by substrates is probably important in the mechanism of action of some oxygenases.

3.2 Electron carrier proteins

Table 3.1 shows some examples of small metalloproteins whose sole redox function is to transfer electrons. Such molecules have proved useful in characterizing the five individual chromophores: haem, 'blue' copper, $Fe_2S_2^*.4CYS$, $Fe_4S_4^*.4CYS$ and Fe.4CYS. These cofactors will be discussed in detail here, and referred to elsewhere in this chapter and the next, as they occur in more complex enzymes or redox systems.

The chromophores are not, of course, merely units slotted into different proteins. We have already noted the influence that the proteins may have on redox potentials, and the mutual effects of protein conformation and metal state on each other. Another problem is that of electron access, especially to enclosed metal sites [44]. Ligands to such metals which are partially exposed to solvent may provide pathways for electron access, for example haem (cytochrome c), HIS (azurin), CYS (ferredoxins), and possibly TYR or TRP. We need not expect these to form stable intermediate redox sites, although in oxidized cytochrome peroxidase, a distinct organic radical is observed

Table 3.1 Molecular properties of some electron carrier proteins

Protein	Mol wt	Cofators
Cytochromes		
c (eucaryotic)	13 000	1 haem b
b_5 (eucaryotic)	11–12 000	1 haem b
c_3 (Desulphovibrio vulgaris)	14 000	4 haem b
Blue copper proteins		
Stellacyanin (lacquer tree)	20 000	1 Cu
Plastocyanin (spinach)	21 000	2 Cu
(French bean)	11 000	1 Cu
Azurin (Pseudomonas, Bordetella)	16 000	1 Cu
Iron-sulphur proteins		
Plant ferredoxin	10 050	1 $Fe_2S_2^*$.4CYS
Adrenodoxin (adrenal P450 complex)	13 090	1 $Fe_2S_2^*$.4CYS
Putidaredoxin (Pseudomonas putida)	12 000	1 $Fe_2S_2^*$.4CYS
Bacterial ferredoxin:		
(Clostridium pasteurianum)	6 000	2 $Fe_4S_4^*$.4CYS
(Desulphovibrio gigas)	6 000	1 $Fe_4S_4^*$.4CYS
HiPIP (Chromatium)	9 600	1 $Fe_4S_4^*$.4CYS
Rubredoxin (Micrococcus aerogenes)	6 380	1 Fe.4CYS
(Pseudomonas oleovorans)	19 000	2 Fe.4CYS

which may represent a 'hopping' site on the electron pathway from cytochrome c to peroxidase haem. Another mechanistic possibility is that an electron may 'tunnel', jumping directly from an enclosed metal past hydrophobic residues to an external redox site.

3.2.1 Cytochromes

Cytochromes of types a, b and c were first characterized spectroscopically in respiring mitochondria, and since then these electron-carrying haemoproteins have proved to very widespread, both at other sites in the eucaryotic cell, and in procaryotes.

Of the various haems (Fig. 3.1), haem b (protohaem) is the commonest, occurring in globins, catalase, peroxidase, cyt b and cyt P450. It can be released from its binding sites, often reversibly, by treatment with acid acetone. There are many soluble procaryotic b cytochromes, and the eucaryotic cyt b_5 is solubilized by enzymatic digestion of microsomes.

c cytochromes contain a covalently bound haem: two CYS residues of the protein chain add across the vinyl groups of haem b. On hydrolysis of the chain, the two CYS residues remain attached to haem by their thioether links, giving haem c. Cyt c ('mammalian') is found generally in eucaryotes, as is cyt c_1 of the respiratory chain. Cyt f from chloroplasts is of the c type, with a rather high E_o' (+ 350 mV). Procaryotic types are very varied: cyt c_2 is similar to cyt c of eucaryotes. (Cyt a and cyt a_3 are components of cytochrome oxidase. Cyt a_3, like cyt P450, has an open-sided haem site, and both are considered in the next chapter.)

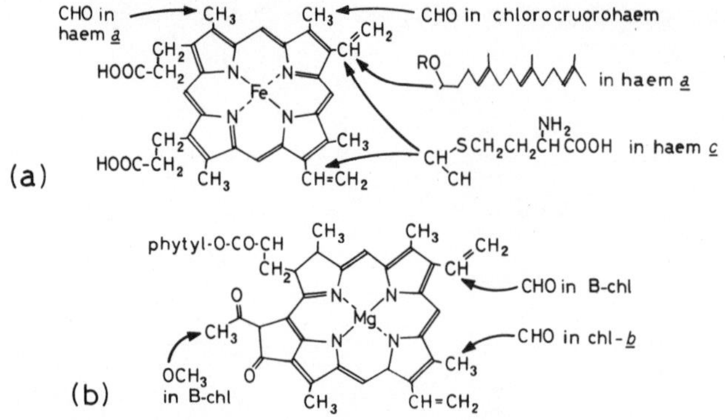

Fig. 3.1 Metal prophyrin complexes. (a) Haem b (protohaem) is the Fe complex of protoporphyrin IX. Substituents are shown for haem a, haem c and chlorocruorohaem (b) Chlorophyll a is a modified Mg-porphyrin. Substituents are shown for chlorophyll b (chl-b) and bacteriochlorophyll (B-chl). *Note:* cytochrome and haem spectra characteristically show α, β and γ (Soret) absorption bands in the visible, of which the α-band is widely used diagnostically. Cytochromes are usually designated by haem type together with a number (b, c_1, a_3 etc.) or the α-wavelength (b-559, c-551 etc.) In the haem-reduced state, the α-bands are in the ranges 550–555 nm (cyt c), 556–558 nm (cyt b) and ca.560 nm (cyt a).

The crystal structures of several cytochromes show haem enclosed in hydrophobic crevices. Protein side-chains supply two axial ligands to Fe so that direct access by small molecules is prevented. With four equatorial N-ligands from porphyrin, Fe has therefore an octahedral hexa-co-ordination. The group alternates between Fe^{II} and Fe^{III} in electron transfer. Because of the enforced hexa-co-ordination, both are low-spin states.

Cyt c has been extensively studied, its sequence used as a phylogenetic marker, and its crystal structure analysed in oxidized and reduced forms from various species [60]. The structure shows haem surrounded by hydrophobic groups with only an edge exposed to solvent. The haem propionate groups hydrogen-bond to internal protein side-chains, and thioether links join the ring to CYS 14 and CYS 17. The two axial ligands are HIS 18 and MET 80, whose bond to Fe is greatly strengthened and shortened in the reduced form. Movements are also evident on the opposite side of haem. Comparison with the structure of cyt c_2 suggests that such induced conformational changes may help control the reactions of cyt c with cyt c_1 and cytochrome oxidase in oxidative phosphorylation, although both reactions are now thought to involve electron transfer across the exposed haem edge rather than through hydrophobic channels.

The structure of cyt b_5 [5], by contrast, shows no change on reduction beyond the binding of a surface cation (which may nevertheless affect protein–protein interactions). As in myoglobin, haem is turned with the propionate chains outward, one of them bending back to be half buried near the Fe atom. As Fe is reduced, a cation approaches this latter carboxylate group anion on the surface of the molecule. The two axial ligands are both HIS. The surface of the protein is largely covered with polar residues, and a hydrophobic tail (which is removed in the proteolytic liberation of cyt b_5) evidently tethers the molecule to the microsomal membrane.

The bacterial cyt c_3 presents an interesting study, with its four haem b per 14000 weight, and its low redox potential ($-200\,\text{mV}$). NMR studies on cyt c_3 from *Desulphovibrio vulgaris* confirm the presence of four haems with axial HIS ligands, and low-spin Fe in both oxidized and reduced forms. The technique also allows the observation of the ten VAL and LEU residues, mainly near haem edges, and twenty LYS mainly on the protein surface [40].

Cytochromes occur in many complex systems as electron shuttles. Apart from the respiratory and photosynthetic pathways, we find cyt b_5 in microsomal, Golgi and outer mitochondrial membrane complexes. Haem groups in complex enzymes are occasionally in enclosed sites (e.g. cyt a), but are usually open-sided.

3.2.2 The blue copper site

The blue copper proteins from plants, algae and bacteria (Table 3.1) contain Cu in an unusual co-ordination site. They transfer electrons at high potential ($+180$ to $+400\,\text{mV}$) using the Cu^I/Cu^{II} couple, and Cu^{II} is characterized by strong visible absorption at 600 nm, and by unusual EPR parameters. The same properties are found in the blue copper oxidases which, in addition, contain other types of Cu. The X-ray structures of plastocyanin ([14], Fig. 3.2) and azurin [4] show that Cu is tetrahedrally co-ordinated with one CYS and two HIS ligands, and a more distant MET. The Cu–S (CYS) distance [66] is

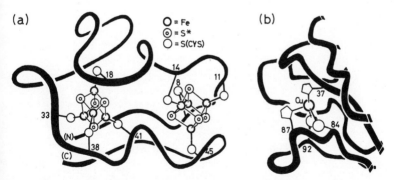

Fig. 3.2 Electron carrier chromophores, from X-ray structures. (a) Ferredoxin (*Micrococcus aerogenes*) showing two Fe–S* clusters bound by eight CYS ligands. (b) Plastocyanin (active site) showing Cu co-ordinated by CYS 84, HIS 37 and 87, and MET 92 (redrawn from [14]).

35

unusually short (210 pm). Stellacyanin, however, contains no MET residues, so that the various blue sites have only some of their ligands in common.

3.2.3 Iron–sulphur proteins

This group (Table 3.1) includes two types of redox carrier that operate at very different potentials. The ferredoxins, found in plants, microorganisms and animals, are reduced at potentials around -420 to -200 mV. On the other hand, the high potential iron proteins (HiPIPs), found in some photosynthetic bacteria, transfer electrons at $+350$ mV. All contain non-haem Fe and sulphide ions in equal proportions. The sulphide is also known as labile sulphur (designated S*) to distinguish it from the covalently bound γ-thiolate of CYS, and it is released as H_2S by acid treatment. Similar groupings are found in the respiratory and photosynthetic electron transfer chains, and appear conjugated to other redox co-factors in enzymes such as xanthine oxidase and nitrogenase.

The usual way to classify iron–sulphur proteins has been by their Fe and labile sulphur content. Thus plant ferredoxin and similar compounds are 2Fe–2S* proteins, HiPIP contains 4Fe–4S*, and bacterial ferredoxin is 8Fe–8S* or occasionally 4Fe–S*. Two simple chromophores have been identified in these carriers, each of which transfers just one electron. The first (almost certainly) is $Fe_2S_2^*.4CYS$, and the second is $Fe_4S_4^*.4CYS$. These represent Fe–S clusters bound to protein through CYS ligation (Fig. 3.2). Plant-type ferredoxins contain $Fe_2S_2^*.4CYS$, while all other carriers contain $Fe_4S_4^*.4CYS$. (Note that although the latter is monovalent in both ferredoxin and HiPIP, it does have more than two accessible oxidation states, and a different choice of couple accounts for the difference of 750 mV in E_o' between the two species.)

The EPR spectra of Fe–S proteins are their most characteristic diagnostic property. At sufficiently low temperatures in the reduced state, all ferredoxins give a signal with $g_{ave} \sim 1.94$, while HiPIP is paramagnetic only in its oxidized state, with $g_{ave} > 2$. Spectroscopy combined with chemical manipulations has assisted in classifying the Fe–S clusters in complex systems [1]. When an Fe–S protein is denatured, for instance in 80% dimethyl sulphoxide, differences in EPR spectra can be correlated with chromophore type. It is assumed that the inorganic clusters remain intact, and the relaxation of protein constraints then allows the signals due to $Fe_2S_2^*$ and $Fe_4S_4^*$ to be distinguished. A second method requires the 'extrusion' of the cluster by thiol reagents such as thiophenol which will displace CYS. Rapid spectrophotometric analysis is then used to distinguish the free anions $Fe_2S_2^*.4RS^-$ and $Fe_4S_4^*.4RS^-$. Such methods have been developed with simple redox carriers for application to complex enzymes, and nitrogenase azoferredoxin, for instance, has been found to yield clusters of the type $Fe_4S_4^*$.

It has long been supposed that the chromophore in *plant-type ferredoxins* is of the form (a):

(a) RS = protein MET or CYS

(b) 2RS =

which is found in model compounds e.g.(b). The oxidized chromophore is red. On reduction, it is bleached and becomes paramagnetic. The $g = 1.94$ EPR signal appears at $77\,K$ for adrenodoxin, and at $10\,K$ for spinach ferredoxin. It is thought that the unpaired spin is delocalized on both Fe and both S* atoms. The oxidized form may be looked on as Fe_2^{III}, and the reduced as $Fe^{III}.Fe^{II}$. In both, the two Fe are spin-coupled: the Fe–Fe distance in the model structure (270 pm) indicates some metal–metal bonding.

Even if all plant-type Fds contain the same co-factor, they involve different apoproteins. The two homologous carriers from P450 complexes (putidaredoxin and adrenodoxin) are unrelated to chloroplast Fd, nor can they be functionally exchanged for it.

The brown *bacterial ferredoxins* are important in a number of reactions, for instance photoreduction and nitrogen fixation. Although among the smallest of proteins, their sequences clearly indicate a gene duplication of a 29-residue fragment. Each half of the molecule contains a similar group of four CYS, and the X-ray structure shows three CYS of one half and one of the other contributing to each of the $Fe_4S_4^*.4CYS$ groups (Fig. 3.2). The sequence of *Desulphoviobrio gigas* Fd seems to have diverged somewhat from this pattern in its C-terminal half, allowing the retention of only one active centre.

It was a considerable surprise when the X-ray structure of HiPIP (whose function is unknown) showed apparently identical Fe–S clusters to those in bacterial Fd. The relation between them is expressed in the 'three-state hypothesis'. The resting states, Fd_{ox} and $HiPIP_{red}$, are thought to share a common electronic state 'C', while Fd_{red} and $HiPIP_{ox}$ represent a reduced and an oxidized form respectively ('C–' and 'C+'). This is paralleled by studies on model compounds of the type $(Et_4N^+)_2(Fe_4S_4(SCH_2Ph)_4)^{2-}$, whose crystal structure closely resembles those of the protein co-factors. Four oxidation states have been demonstrated in the model systems, whose properties can be matched with those of the proteins:

	C⁻ state	C state	C⁺ state
	$[Fe_4S_4(SR)_4]^{4-} \rightleftharpoons$	$[Fe_4S_4(SR)_4]^{3-} \rightleftharpoons$	$[Fe_4S_4(SR)_4]^{2-} \rightleftharpoons$ $[Fe_4S_4(SR)_4]^{1-}$
		$Fd_{red} \rightleftharpoons$	Fd_{ox} (? $\rightleftharpoons$ Fd_{s-ox})
		$HiPIP_{s-red} \rightleftharpoons$	$HiPIP_{red} \rightleftharpoons$ $HiPIP_{ox}$
Formal oxidation level:		$3Fe^{II}Fe^{III}$	$2Fe^{II}2Fe^{III}$ $Fe^{II}3Fe^{III}$

There is evidence for the super-reduced ('s-red') HiPIP and a suggestion of the super-oxidized Fd. An important feature of these model studies is that they allow the determination of the overall charge of the C-state species. This is almost impossible simply by studying the chromophores in the protein environment.

The crystal structures of oxidized and reduced HiPIP show a slight shrinkage and distortion of the inorganic cluster on oxidation, with no major conformational change. Similar results are reported for Fd. There is no indication from these studies why HiPIP does not normally assume a $C-$ state, nor Fd $C+$. The chromophores in each case are surrounded by non-polar side-chains, with slightly more solvent access in the latter. Electron transfer could take place via CYS ligands: sequence studies show that TYR is not involved as had once been thought.

Although they have no labile sulphur, the *rubredoxins* are included among the Fe–S proteins, as they have many properties in common. The chromophore Fe.4CYS (which has not been found elsewhere) contains Fe tetrahedrally co-ordinated by CYS, and the Fe^{II}/Fe^{III} couple acts at $-60\,mV$. A unique feature of the structure is one very short $Fe^{III}-S$ bond of 205 pm. (The others are 224–234 pm.) The role of rubredoxin is unknown, but a larger 2Fe protein from *Pseudomonas oleovorans* supplies electrons for hydroxylations.

3.3 Some enzymes containing molybdenum, cobalt and iron

We now turn to some examples of open-sided metal sites. The Mo-enzymes are good examples of the coupling of such sites to electron flow from electron transfer groups: they all contain Mo together with at least one other redox co-factor. The chemical nature of cobalamin-dependent enzymes puts them alongside redox enzymes, even though the reactions catalysed often simply amount to carbon-skeletal rearrangements. We also describe some functionally related Fe-enzymes.

3.3.1 Molybdenum

Biological Mo [3] is less well understood then Fe or Cu in redox catalysis. Both chemically and spectroscopically it has proved difficult to characterize, but its role in nitrogen fixation has attracted great interest. Table 3.2 shows that it also occurs in a mitochondrial haemoprotein and a group of flavoproteins. Together with other metals, it is very important in the metabolism of oxyanions of N and S, which act both as electron sinks for respiration and as sources of the elements in available form for cellular reactions.

Only one *nitrogenase* enzyme seems to have evolved, common to both bacteria and blue-green algae. It has two components, known as azoferredoxin and molybdoferredoxin (Table 3.2). Azoferredoxin contains some $Fe_4S_4^*$ (p. 36), while a co-factor (mol wt 2000) has been isolated from molybdoferredoxin containing Mo and Fe–S* [3].

Table 3.2 Molecular properties of some molybdenum enzymes

Enzyme	Mol wt	Mo	flavin	Fe, S
Nitrogenase:				
azoferredoxin	$2 \times 27\,500$	–	–	8 Fe–8S*
molybdoferredoxin	$2 \times 50\,700 + 2 \times 59\,500$	2	–	22–24(Fe–S*)
Xanthine oxidase	275 000 (dimer)	2	2 FAD	8Fe–8S*
Nitrate reductase	1 000 000	1	? FMN	40(Fe–S*)
Sulphite oxidase	110 000 (dimer)	2	–	2 cyt b

The two components probably combine in the ratio of $2:1$ in the nitrogen fixation reaction:

Bacterial Fd receives electrons from a variety of sources (H_2/hydrogenase, pyruvate dehydrogenase or photoreduction, for instance) and transfers them to azoferredoxin. The electrons are then passed on to molybdoferredoxin in an ATP-dependent reaction ($1e^-:1ATP$). This step probably represents an energy transduction in which electrons are forced to the low potentials necessary to reduce N_2. Molybdoferredoxin accumulates the requisite number of electrons for this (six), and it is also capable of reducing a number of other substrates such as acetylene and nitriles. In addition, H_2 may be evolved reversibly, apparently at a different enzymatic site. However, H_2 cannot serve to reduce N_2 without the intervention of the hydrogenase-Fd system. Its formation decreases with N_2-reduction, and probably results from an overspill of excess reducing power.

There is no direct evidence on how N_2 is activated, although the chemical properties of Mo make it a very likely candidate for a catalyst in the reaction. (The mechanistic problem in N_2 fixation is that although overall reduction to aqueous ammonia is exothermic, the formation of likely intermediates such as $HN{=}NH$ and $H_2N{-}NH_2$ is not.) Two Mo atoms, using their oxidation states $+3$ to $+6$ could, in principle, supply six electrons rapidly to N_2.

Three similar enzymes are involved in oxidizing aldehydes and purines: xanthine oxidase, xanthine dehydrogenase and aldehyde oxidase (Table 3.2). Probably two identical subunits each contain Mo, flavin (FAD) and two distinct $Fe_2S_2^*$ centres. The activity of xanthine oxidase involves the liberation of either peroxide or superoxide in the course of oxidizing the organic substrate, and experiments with a deflavo-enzyme indicate that FAD actually binds and reduces O_2. Mo and the Fe–S* groups are involved in catalytic electron transfer, and a protein disulphide is also implicated in the mechanism of action.

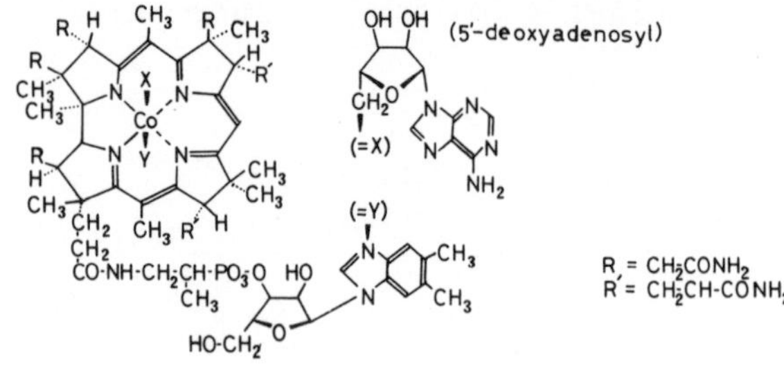

Fig. 3.3 Derivatives of vitamin B_{12}. The *corrin* ring system contains Co co-ordinated by four equatorial N-atoms. One axial position (Y) is taken by a side-chain of the ring. *Cobamides* have various Y-substituents attached to ribose. The example shown is derived from α-(5,6 dimethylbenzimidazolyl) cobamide, or *cobalamin*. In coenzyme B_{12} X is adenosyl, (shown), with a Co—C bond. Other cobalamins are B_{12a} (X = H_2O, Co^{III}) and the vitamin itself, cyanocobalamin (X = CN, Co^{III}).

3.3.2 Cobalt

The corrin ring derivatives (Fig. 3.3) have provided a wealth of metal–organic chemistry which has helped to illuminate the properties of the Vitamin B_{12}-dependent enzymes. The latter fall into two groups: those thought to involve H-transfer, and those involved in methyl-group transfer.

In the first group of enzymes, the active form of the corrin system is known to be 5'-deoxyadenosyl cobalamin. An example of the reaction type is shown below for methylmalonyl-CoA mutase:

This particular enzyme is important in propionate metabolism both for animals and micro-organisms. Other enzymes in the group catalyse similar rearrangements in amino-acids, amines and alcohols. The mechanism involves abstraction of H from substrate by the coenzyme: this H-atom is commonly found to have equilibrated with the two 5'-H atoms on the deoxyadenosyl group. Substrate rearrangement then takes place, and H is returned to its new position. (The ribonucleotide reductases, to be described later, present a special case in which H is transferred from one substrate to another.)

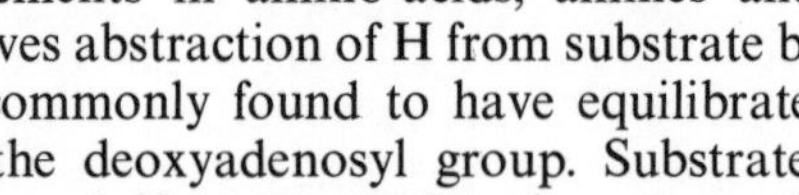

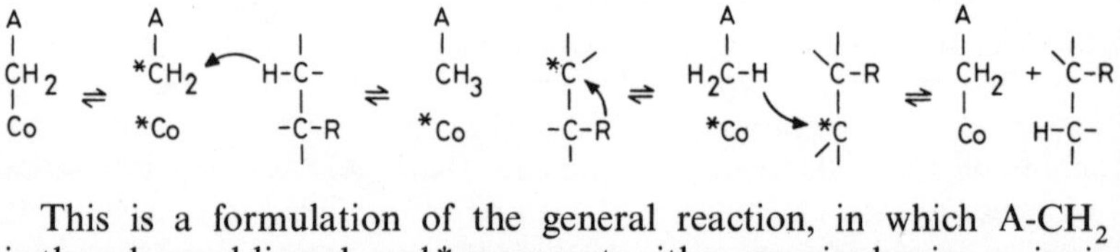

This is a formulation of the general reaction, in which A-CH_2 is the adenosyl ligand, and * represents either unpaired spins or ionic charges generated by the homolysis or heterolysis of the Co–C bond

40

prior to reaction with substrate. Fission of this bond is implicated in enzyme action, and in some systems EPR spectra of Co^{II} and an organic free radical may be observed. However, this does not exclude the possibility that the actual catalytic species is Co^{III}–carbanion or Co^{I}–carbonium formed in equilibrium with the free radical. In fact such variation of the Co leaving-group may be a facet of the action of the B_{12} coenzyme.

The second group of B_{12} enzymes perform methyl transfer, including the synthesis of acetate, methane and methionine, and probably the bacterial conversion of Hg^{2+} to methyl mercury. They all utilize methylated corrin derivatives as intermediates.

Methionine synthetase, the best characterized example, is found in birds, mammals and bacteria. It requires S-adenosyl methionine, reduced flavin, and 1,4-dithiothreitol for initial methylation, and for the reversal of oxidative inactivation during reaction. Its action is to transfer a methyl group from N^5-methyltetrahydrofolate to homocysteine, and its absence may be a prime factor in the pathology of pernicious anaemia.

3.3.3 Ribonucleotide reductases

The reduction of ribonucleotide phosphates to the 2′-deoxy form is an essential step in the formation of DNA, and hence in cell replication. Enzymes involving either cobalamin or Fe co-factors [32] perform a reaction in which the 2′–OH of ribose is replaced by H with retention of configuration: no other substituents are affected. Reducing equivalents for the reaction are transferred from NADPH by a specific flavoprotein to *thioredoxin*, an acidic protein of weight 12 000 containing a reducible disulphide.

While Fe-enzymes have been isolated from animals, plants and bacteria, B_{12} ribonucleotide reductases have been found only in microorganisms. Not surprisingly, all the enzymes are subject to various allosteric controls by the oxy- and deoxy-ribonucleotides. The thioredoxin molecules for the Co and Fe enzymes are similar but not interchangeable.

B_{12} enzymes are known which are specific either for nucleoside diphosphate or triphosphate reduction. The best known is one of the latter, from *Lactobacillus leichmannii*. The mechanism proposed is based on homolytic Co–C cleavage:

The Co^{II} formed by homolysis is omitted throughout the scheme, and $Th(SH)_2$ represents the thioredoxin molecule.

The Fe enzyme from *E.coli* is constituted from two subunits, each dimeric. One contains two Fe atoms which are essential for the catalytic activity of the holoprotein, while the other apparently contains two types of nucleotide effector site. An EPR signal, which depends on the presence of the Fe co-factor, is correlated with the activity of the enzyme. However, it is not that of Fe. The latter has a Mossbauer spectrum very similar to haemerythrin, suggesting that two high-spin Fe^{III} are adjacent and spin-coupled. The implication of a radical species in the mechanism is consistent with a mechanism like that proposed for the B_{12} enzyme. The role of the possible Fe_2 group is not obvious, unless it reduces O_2 to superoxide for subsequent H-atom abstraction and radical formation.

3.4 Electron transfer in respiration and photosynthesis

We have seen how the metal chromophores which occur in small mobile redox carriers are used as units in electron transfer chains. The carriers often occur as components of enzyme complexes, for instance the cyt b_5 or ferredoxin molecules which feed electrons to cyt P450. The chromophores themselves, especially the Fe−S* groups, are used repeatedly, conjugated to other groups within complex enzymes. In either situation, such intermediate carriers may play a role in ensuring specificity or control of reaction, as well as speeding electron transport by providing an evenly graded series of redox potentials.

The most elaborate and important redox transfer chains are those associated with photosynthesis and respiration. While 2-electron oxidases and enzymes like nitrate reductase may have served early roles in removing O_2 and disposing of electrons, respectively, the coupling of oxidative reactions to phosphorylation was an evolutionary breakthrough. First (presumably) in photosynthesis, then in oxidative phosphorylation, electron transport down a series of electron carriers of graded potential was coupled to the phosphorylation of ADP. In each case membraneous arrays of complex enzymes and small carriers allowed the energy of a vigorous oxidation reaction to be converted into a chemical form (ATP) which could be utilized throughout the cell.

Keilin, in his classical optical studies, characterized three types of cytochrome at work in *mitochondrial respiration*. In the last 20 years an additional, unsuspected range of new chromophores (the Fe−S* centres) have been shown by EPR spectroscopy to be involved in the same processes. Fig. 3.4 shows the principal respiratory particles assembled in complete chains for the oxidation of NADH and succinate. The actual electron flow is more complicated than shown, and no doubt more redox centres await identification.

Complexes I and II contain covalently bound flavin groups which dehydrogenate NADH and succinate, splitting the resultant electron pairs. Single electrons are then passed on to various Fe−S* centres

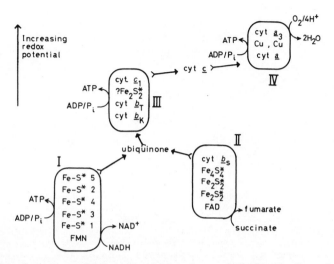

Fig. 3.4 Components of the mitochondrial respiratory chain. Complex I contains five centres which are thought to be of the $Fe_2S_2^*$ type. Complex II is tentatively described as containing two $Fe_2S_2^*$ centres and one of HiPIP type. Complex III contains two cyt b and one cyt c, as well as an $Fe_2S_2^*$ centre. Complex IV, cytochrome oxidase, is the only defined enzyme in the system, containing 2 Cu and 2 haem a (see Chapter 4).

of increasing E_o'. They are paired for transport by quinone, then pass singly again to cytochrome oxidase (see next chapter).

In the 'light phase' of *photosynthesis*, the reaction centres of chloroplasts (and the membranes of photosynthetic micro-organisms) receive energy which has been absorbed by chlorophyll (p. 20). In the 'dark phase', which concerns us here, the energy is used to drive endothermic redox reactions. In the scheme of Hill and Bendall, one reaction centre in chloroplasts (I) is used to reduce $NADP^+$ to NADPH for synthetic use, while another (II) abstracts electrons from water with the liberation of O_2. Electrons are then passed from system I to system II along a transfer chain with concurrent phosphorylation of ADP to ATP. Bacteria were assumed to lack photosystem II, thus needing exogenous reducing agents such as H_2S to feed electrons into the chain. A cyclic reaction is possible in which the products of photosystem I are allowed to react together through the chain. This produces ATP, but no NADPH. The cyclic reaction is induced artificially by adding electron carriers such as ferricyanide, but may also have some physiological importance for bacteria.

When energy is absorbed by either photosystem, a photodonor and a photoacceptor react to give active oxidized and reduced species, respectively. The photodonor of system II, which in its oxidized form abstracts electrons from water to give O_2, contains Mn, though its biochemical form is unknown.

Fig. 3.5 shows a simple scheme for electron transfer in chloroplasts. It can be seen that b and c cytochromes, a quinone, Fe–S* centres

43

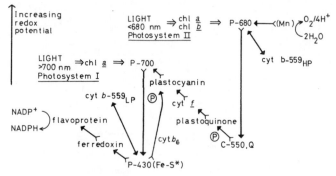

Fig. 3.5 Components of the chloroplast electron transfer chain. There are three spectroscopic species of cytochrome: b-563 ($= b_6$), c-554 ($= f$) and b-559 which has high and low potential forms ($E_0' = +370$ and $+70$ mV). The photodonors P-680 and P-700 are pairs of modified chlorophyll a. Q and C-550 (a carotenoid) are the photoacceptors of system II, while P-430 of system I is associated with two membrane-bound Fe–S* centres (E_0' -600 and -500 mV). ⓟ represents possible sites of coupled phosphorylation. See note to Fig. 3.1.

and a flavoprotein participate, all reminiscent of the mitochondrial respiratory chain. In addition there is the blue Cu–protein plastocyanin, and chlorophyll molecules of various types. Non-cyclic electron flow is shown, and also a cyclic flow mediated by cyt b_6 (but not the artificially induced cyclic flow). Many chromophores have not yet been chemically identified, and the pathways are more complex than those shown. No role for cyt b_{559}, for instance, has yet been determined.

Figs. 3.4 and 3.5 demonstrate the considerable part played by metal co-factors in electron transport, with the precise control that can be exerted over their redox potentials. Another important feature of the chains lies in the alternation of hydride and electron transport (i.e. of organic and metal redox carriers). Where a membrane is spanned by electron transfer chains, and also contains a mobile hydride carrier (B), then thermal diffusion of B and BH_2 across the membrane, together with electron flow along the chains, provides a simple proton pump:

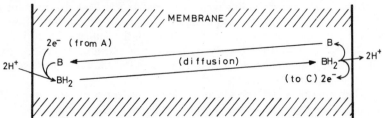

Here A and C represent the termini of electron transport chains. In the chemiosmotic hypothesis, it is the resulting protonmotive force that is responsible for driving both phosphorylation of ADP and other processes.

Broadly speaking, the redox transfer centres are used at increasing redox potential in the order flavin, Fe–S*, quinone, cyt b cyt c, Cu, cyt a. Cu plays only a small part, and in Chapter 1 we suggested a historical reason why this might be so. Chemically, the Cu-proteins only act in the moderate to high range of E_o' (ca. + 200 to + 800 mV), and a Cu electron carrier able to act at lower potentials would require a novel Cu co-ordination. However Cu oxidases might conceivably have evolved instead of cytochrome oxidase in bacteria, had Cu been more abundant, and they do play a similar role in plants.

4 Dealing with oxygen

Oxygen is a powerful oxidant, yet it is kinetically inert. This paradox has allowed life, in evolution, to come to terms with oxygen in the atmosphere, and to make controlled use of it in biosynthesis, biodegradation and respiration. The twin problems for survival are to activate oxygen sufficiently for reaction, while ensuring that dangerous by-products are not allowed to damage the organism. In this chapter we shall see that metals (almost exclusively Fe and Cu) are used to deal with oxygen, superoxide and peroxide. Flavin is the only organic co-factor known to interact enzymatically with oxygen.

Table 4.1 shows the principal physiological reactions of di-oxygen species. After considering the activation and toxicity of oxygen, we go on to consider the individual proteins concerned in its metabolism. Three metal groupings – haem, Fe_2 and Cu_2 – turn out to be surprisingly versatile in these reactions.

Table 4.1 Biological conversions of dioxygen species

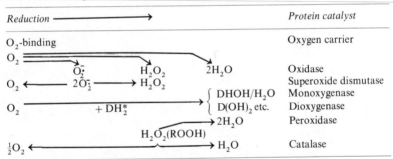

Notes: $pK_a(HO_2^-) = 4.45$, $pK_a(H_2O_2) = 11.62$. *Oxygenation substrate.

4.1 The activation and toxicity of oxygen

The kinetic inertness of oxygen is emphasized by the fact that autoxidation of organic compounds (i.e. reaction with O_2) at room temperature usually only takes place with metal-ion catalysis, by photochemical activation (e.g. of butadienes). or by chain reactions promoted by an extraneous radical (e.g. of ethers). Simple bimolecular reactions between O_2 and organic compounds are unusual. This situation may be understood in terms of two factors: the high energy of formation of superoxide, and the stability of triplet O_2 (Fig. 4.1). One-electron reduction

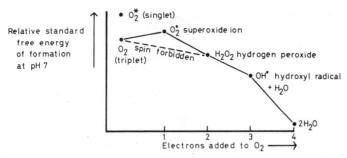

Fig. 4.1 Thermodynamics of dioxygen reduction. E'_0 for a couple is represented by the slope of the line joining the two species. An intermediate can only disproportionate to the two species if it lies above such a line.

of O_2 to superoxide ion is thermodynamically unfavourable, requiring a reducing couple of $-330\,mV$. Reduction to any other species is exothermic, but now we encounter a spin restriction. O_2 has a 'triplet' ground state, with two unpaired electron spins. Quantum mechanical laws require that if it is to be rapidly reduced to peroxide, a diamagnetic ('singlet') molecule, then the reductant supplying the two electrons must be a free radical, or must change from a singlet to a triplet state, or O_2 itself must be excited to its singlet state. This rules out most stable organic substrates, since organic free radicals are generally unstable. Two-electron reduction of O_2 by singlet molecules, being spin-forbidden, will not take place in the lifetime of a simple collision-complex (ca. $10^{-13}\,s$).

However, to emphasis the sluggish nature of O_2 in many reactions is not to deny its toxicity to aerobic as well as anaerobic organisms [31]. Transition metals react with O_2 in various ways by virtue of their labile d-electron configurations. (Flavin, by contrast, probably activates O_2 by adopting a semiquinone radical state.) If Cu or Fe salts are added to tissue slices or cultures, they promote O_2-toxicity, while *in vivo* they are pressed into service as co-factors to control its reactions, and destroy its dangerous by-products.

An important agent of O_2-toxicity is thought to be the superoxide ion [3], which may be formed by the uncontrolled autoxidation of low-potential cytochromes, iron–sulphur proteins and flavoproteins, as well as by the decomposition of complexes like oxyhaemoglobin. Superoxide and its conjugate acid are powerful reagents, capable either of reduction to peroxide, or oxidation to O_2 (see Fig. 4.1). Oxidation of organic material by superoxide may be unspecific, involving H-atom abstraction and yielding autoxidizable radicals. In addition, the spontaneous disproportionation of superoxide yields singlet O_2 and peroxide, while its reaction with peroxide gives a hydroxyl radical. (Both singlet O_2 and hydroxyl radical are more destructive than superoxide, though their importance *in vivo* has not been demonstrated.) The classic example of a flavoprotein oxidase which

47

reduces O_2 to superoxide by a one-electron reduction is xanthine oxidase – up to one third of O_2 consumed under experimental conditions is liberated as superoxide. It is suggested that the bacteriostatic action of milk xanthine oxidase is due to the production of superoxide and hydroxyl radicals, while superoxide is also implicated in the bacteriocidal activity of granular leucocytes [6]. Peroxidases in similar circumstances (p. 58) also have a bacteriocidal effect, by direct oxidation.

Anaerobic organisms may display some defence against O_2. They usually possess enzymes which can consume O_2 to some extent, so that its presence may merely inhibit growth by diverting normal metabolism into defensive O_2-consumption. However, incomplete reduction of O_2 leading to the formation of the various more destructive chemical species may occur, and the degree of O_2-tolerance of a number of anaerobes has been correlated with their superoxide dismutase activity [46]. Catalase may also be important.

The erythrocyte is an example of an aerobic cell which requires a robust defence against the damaging effects of O_2. O_2, attacking the polyunsaturated fatty acids in the cell membrane, produces hydroperoxides which must be reduced by glutathione in the presence of glutathione peroxidase. In addition, oxyhaemoglobin slowly decomposes to give superoxide and methaemoglobin. Superoxide is converted by erythrocuprein (superoxide dismutase) to O_2 and peroxide, and the latter is destroyed by glutathione peroxidase or catalase. Methaemoglobin (comprising 1% human haemoglobin) is reduced to deoxyhaemoglobin by a pathway involving cytochrome b_5. Thus in this case we see one Cu/Zn-protein and three haemoproteins guarding against superoxide and peroxides, while a fourth binds O_2 reversibly.

4.2 Oxygen carriers

The saturated concentration of O_2 in pure water at atmospheric pressure is about 0.3 mM. The effect of haemoglobin (Hb) circulating in human blood is to provide a reliable uptake of O_2 in the lungs (to 9 mM overall) together with efficient unloading in the body where it is most needed. The co-operative properties of the Hb molecule, manifested in its familiar sigmoid O_2-saturation curve ensure that while saturation in the lungs is not much affected by variation in loading pressure (pO_2 ca. 100 mm Hg), unloading in the tissues at 40 mm Hg or less is very sensitive to local anoxia. In strenuous exercise, the overall unloading of O_2 may reach 85%.

Animals have many specialized requirements for O_2 transport and storage, depending on the loading and unloading pressures of O_2, and a range of respiratory pigments (oxygen carriers) appear in the tissues as well for buffering vascular O_2-supply. The lugworm actually stores O_2 in its blood. At high tide, plasma O_2-solubility alone is adequate for supplying body tissues, and only at low tide does hypoxia lead to the unloading of O_2 from circulating Hb. Again, diving mam-

Table 4.2 Molecular properties of some oxygen carriers

Protein	Mol wt	Co-factors
Myoglobin	17 500	1 haem b
Haemoglobin	64 500 ($\alpha_2\beta_2$)	4 haem b
Haemocyanin – functional subunits:		
arthropod	70–75 000	2 Cu
mollusc	48–52 000	2 Cu
Haemerythrin	8 × 13 500	8 × 2 Fe

mals need high capacity for storing O_2, while the mammalian foetus must cope with a low loading pressure in the placenta.

Three series of O_2-carrier molecules are known in animals, based on haem, Cu and non-haem Fe cofactors (Table 4.2). The physiological needs of invertebrates are satisfied in diverse and apparently haphazard fashion by these types. Haem proteins are widespread in annelids, crustaceans and molluscs, and are represented in insects and nematodes. (They also occur in yeasts, moulds, and leguminous plants root nodules.) Chlorocruorin, based on a different porphyrin (Fig. 3.1), is found only in annelids. While vertebrate haemoproteins are intracellular, invertebrate Hb is found in body fluids, as well as in erythrocytes, coelomic corpuscles and other tissues. Extracellular Hb (erythrocruorin) is often polymeric, reaching weights of over 10^6. Haemocyanin is found in arthropods and molluscs, haemerythrin among sipunculids, polychaete annelids, priapulids and brachiopods.

It is the rule rather than the exception that these pigments are polymorphic within an animal. Just as humans have several normal Hb chains, and a related muscle protein (myoglobin), so different haemerythrins may occur in the coelom, haemolymph and muscle of invertebrates. Fish blood contains Hb types of differing pH sensitivity, allowing differential supply to the swim bladder and the body in general. As a further variation, some animals manifest pigments with different co-factors, occasionally even within the same cell.

The existence of vanadium-containing cells in the blood of certain annelid marine worms has raised the interesting possibility of a respiratory pigment containing vanadium. These 'vanadocytes', which have green vacuoles containing V^{III} or V^{IV} and sulphuric acid both in about molar concentration, were thought to be involved in O_2 transport and storage. However, this has now been disproved [39]. Such organisms may, in fact, be too sluggish to require a specific circulating O_2 carrier.

4.2.1 Myoglobin and haemoglobin

These homologous proteins, containing haem b (Fig. 3.1), have provided a testing ground for a number of biophysical techniques and theories of protein action. We shall only try to draw a few strands from material which has been thoroughly covered elsewhere.

Myoglobin (Mb), a monomeric muscle O_2-storage protein, contains ferrous haem b (Mb[II]), and reacts reversibly with O_2 to form oxy-myoglobin (MbO$_2$). It can be oxidized to an inactive ferrihaem form, metmyoglobin (Mb[III]). Hb is analogous except that, having four subunits, fully saturated HbO$_2$ in fact contains four O_2 molecules.

The conclusions of magnetic studies on Mb and Hb are that the deoxy (Fe[II]) forms are high-spin complexes, while Mb[III] and Hb[III] are equilibrium mixtures of high- and low-spin forms. In the high-spin species, Fe is five co-ordinate with an axial HIS ligand. Fe in Hb[II] is thought to be displaced towards HIS by between 20 pm [18] and 63 pm [52]. In the low-spin species, Fe lies in the haem plane, and a second axial ligand is accepted to complete a hexa-co-ordination. We may speculate that O_2 approaches the open side of haem in Mb[II], forming a loose complex with some spin-pairing, and the Fe then moves into the haem plane to form the fully spin-paired MbO$_2$, which may have one of the following structures:

$$\text{(a)} \quad \text{M-O-O} \qquad \text{(b)} \quad \text{M-O}^{\diagup \text{O}} \qquad \text{(c)} \quad \text{M}\diagdown^{\text{O}}_{\text{O}}$$

Theoretical studies suggest that O_2 will not bind to metal in linear fashion (a), but might form a bent (b) or perpendicular (c) configuration, as found in various inorganic superoxide and peroxide compounds, respectively. Structure (b) is favoured by the observed O—O stretching frequency of HbO$_2$, and is found in the structure of a model oxyhaem ('picket fence') compound. A recent crystallographic study [52] supports its occurrence in MbO$_2$. The Fe atom is ferrous in character, and MbO$_2$ and HbO$_2$ are best thought of as non-ionic Fe[II] $- O_2$ compounds, analogous to the metal carbonyls. It is the relative stability of the metal–O_2 bond, rather than the non-polar nature of the haem crevice, that tends to prevent decomposition to superoxide and haem.[III].

Tetrameric human Hb has two pairs of subunits (Table 4.2) which bind four O_2 molecules. At least three factors control the O_2 affinity of Hb, and they all operate through changes of tertiary and quaternary structure. They are: co-operation between subunits, binding of protons, and binding of phosphates. They can be thought of as mediating physiological responses to loading and unloading pressures, local pH, and diphosphoglycerate levels, respectively. Binding of O_2, for instance, locks haem into a low-spin state, and the resultant shifts in Fe, axial HIS, and other parts of the porphyrin ring (which may move by more than 30 pm) affect the local globin structure. These changes are transmitted by subunit interactions to the other haems, increasing their O_2 affinity by favouring their low-spin conformations. Conversely, information passed from deoxygenated sites will tend to destabilize the low-spin oxy and deoxy-states with respect to the high-spin deoxy state in other haems, favouring release of O_2. The binding of protons and phosphates have a similar allosteric effect in tending to reverse O_2

binding. In active muscle, for instance, where CO_2 and lactic acid are entering the plasma and liberating protons, the unloading of O_2 is enhanced. Diphosphoglycerate is an intermediate in glycolysis which is particularly abundant in erythrocytes [9]. In conditions of prolonged hypoxia (e.g. at high altitudes) its concentration increases. Because of the shape of the Hb O_2-saturation curve, O_2-affinity is more affected at low pressures (in the tissues) than at high (in the lungs), so that the net effect is to improve distribution to the body.

4.2.2 Haemocyanin

Haemocyanins (Hcn) vary in their degree of aggregation between species, some reaching weights of 10^7. They contain strongly bound Cu atoms which appear, from stoichiometry and magnetic properties, to act in pairs. Both O_2 and CO bind reversibly in the ratio 1 (O_2, CO) :2 (Cu). While the apoprotein and CO-complex are colourless, $HcnO_2$ is blue, with absorption bands at 362 and 680 nm, and is believed to have a peroxide-like structure:

$$\text{Hcn } (Cu_2^I) + O_2 \rightleftharpoons \text{Hcn } (Cu_2^{II} O_2^{2-})$$

The Cu content differs between molluscs and arthropods, but in each case one O_2 is reversibly bound per Cu_2. The two phyla also show different quaternary forms of the protein under the electron microscope. The mollusc Hcn subunit contains 18–20 O_2-binding sites, and forms pentameric discs. These stack into cylinders with five-fold symmetry. Arthropod Hcn, on the other hand, has a monomer which also appears in dimers, tetramers and octamers. The monomers can be dissociated into six functional units (mol wt 75 000), each containing Cu_2. The equivalent weight per Cu_2 in mollusc Hcn is 50 000, containing two equal protein chains. It is proposed that the 2-Cu unit is similar in both forms, while arthropod Hcn contains an additional structural protein chain.

4.2.3 Haemerythrin

Like the vertebrate globins, haemerythrin (Hrn) is intracellular, has a related monomeric muscle protein, and elsewhere is oligomeric (usually octameric, rarely trimeric). It has a high content of α-helix: four near-parallel rods surround an active site, which contains two Fe atoms, in each subunit [34].

Colourless Hrn binds one O_2 per Fe_2 to give $HrnO_2$, which has an unusual reddish-violet colour. Extensive physical studies have shown that Hrn contains two high-spin Fe^{II} ions, while $HrnO_2$ is essentially a diferric peroxide (cf. $HcnO_2$). The high-spin Fe^{III} ions in $HrnO_2$, probably bridged by an oxide ion, are spin-coupled: this is consistent with the X-ray Fe–Fe distance of 344 pm. The pair of Fe atoms lies parallel to a surrounding ring of four HIS ligands, one from each helical rod. The ring lies between the four rods, approximately perpendicular to them. On one side of the ring are further ligands from the protein chain, TYR and possibly carboxyl and amide groups, drawing the Fe pair slightly out of the plane of the HIS ring. The opposite open side of the ring is the binding site for O_2.

4.3 Superoxide dismutases

In view of the destructive properties of superoxide, it is no surprise that highly efficient enzymes have evolved which disproportionate the molecule into O_2 and peroxide. Three distinct enzymes have been characterized, containing as co-factors $Cu + Zn$, Fe and Mn (see Table 4.3, and also p. 13). Chemically, any redox couple is adequate for this catalytic role with a potential between that of O_2^-/H_2O_2 ($+ 300$ mV) and that of O_2/O_2^- ($- 300$ mV), and with little metal affinity for O_2 or HO_2^-.

Erythrocuprein in erythrocytes, like ceruloplasmin in plasma, was originally thought simply to be a Cu-sequestering protein. It has now been shown to be an effective cytoplasmic superoxide dismutase, identical to similar proteins elsewhere (hepatocuprein, cerebrocuprein).

The two protein sites are thought not to interact with each other, and each contains 1 Cu + 1 Zn bridged by an HIS ligand ([57], Table 2.1 and Fig. 2.1). The Cu co-ordination is approximately square planar, with solvent access to one axial position.

The Fe and Mn series of enzymes are homologous in sequence, but unrelated to the cupreins. Bacteria may elaborate both Fe and Mn types, while chicken liver yields a cytoplasmic cuprein and a mitochondrial Mn enzyme. The mechanism of action is presumably one of alternate oxidation and reduction of Cu: that of the others may be the same, although a more complex set of oxidation states has been proposed for Mn.

Table 4.3 Molecular properties of superoxide dismutases

Source	Mol wt	Co-factors
Source	33 000 (dimer)	2 (Cu + Zn)
Chicken liver mitochondria	80 000 (tetramer)	2.3 Mn
Bacteria	38 700 (dimer)	1.02 Fe
Bacteria	40 000 (dimer)	1.2 Mn
Blue-green algae	36 500 (dimer)	0.94 Fe

4.4 Oxidases

Table 4.4 shows some enzymes which reduce O_2 to water or peroxide. The most important of the four-electron oxidases is cytochrome oxidase, the terminal oxidase in the mitochondrial and some procaryotic respiratory electron transfer chains. (In micro-organisms a related cytochrome a_1 is also found in this role, as are cytochromes a_2 ($= d$) and o, containing a substituted chlorohaem and haem b respectively.) Ascorbate oxidase, one of the three 'blue' oxidases, has been assigned a corresponding terminal oxidase role in some plants, while laccase

Table 4.4 Molecular properties of some oxidases

Enzyme	Mol wt	Co-factors
4-electron oxidases*		
Cytochrome c oxidase	100–180 000	2 Cu, 2 haem a
Laccase (lacquer tree)	64 000	4 Cu
(fungus)	110 000	4 Cu
Ceruloplasmin	132 000	6–7 Cu
Ascorbate oxidase	132 000	8 Cu
2-electron oxidases[†]		
Benzylamine oxidase	195 000	2 Cu, 2 pyridoxal
Uricase	120 000	1 Cu
Many Flavoproteins		FMN, FAD

Notes: *$O_2 \rightarrow 2H_2O$ [†]$O_2 \rightarrow H_2O_2$.

oxidase oxidizes organic substrates directly.

The very efficiency with which these enzymes reduce O_2 to water makes their mechanisms difficult to study. Here the structural analogies with other Fe and Cu proteins provides a useful basis for interpreting reactions. In this context we may mention that P_7 peroxidase and tyrosinase, both mixed-function oxygenases, are capable of four-electron oxidase activity, but in two (at least) distinct steps.

Many two-electron oxidases are flavoproteins, but plasma benzylamine oxidase exemplifies a widespread group of Cu- and pyridoxal phosphate-containing amine oxidases. Like the flavoprotein monoamine oxidase, they catalyse oxidative deaminations:

$$R - CH_2 - NH_2 + O_2 + H_2O \rightarrow R - CHO + H_2O_2 + NH_3.$$

The lysine oxidase essential for cross-linking elastin and collagen in connective tissue belongs to this group. Other mitochondrial and microsomal metalloproteins act as two-electron oxidases, and 5–15% of liver O_2 consumption leads to such peroxide formation. The resultant peroxides are then utilized by hydroperoxidases.

4.4.1 Cytochrome oxidase
This is a mitochondrial membrane-bound lipoprotein, containing equal amounts of Cu and haem a. It can be solubilized with detergents or bile salts, but tends to aggregate in solution. It is composed of at least ten subunits, some of mitochondrial and others of cytoplasmic origin. Some cardiolipin is essential for activity, and lipid may represent up to 30% of the enzyme weight as purified. Although the haem groups are chemically identical, it is considered that they occur in two different environments. For this reason, the enzyme is referred to as a complex of cytochromes a and a_3. These have not been separated in any active form, but provide convenient labels for the two haem sites.

Oxidized cyt $a.a_3$ is fully reduced by four electrons. On the basis of optical and magnetic studies, cyt a resembles cyt c, while cyt a_3

is more like Mb. That is to say, cyt a is a closed site involved only in electron transfer, while cyt a_3 is thought to be open-sided, with varying spin-states, and is able to react with O_2. Electrons are supplied by cyt c to cyt a, and passed on via the 2 Cu to cyt a_3 where they reduce O_2 to water. The mechanism of reduction of O_2 by cyt a_3 may be as follows:

$$Fe^{III}(cyt\ a_3)\ \xleftarrow{\hspace{6cm}(low\text{-}spin)\hspace{6cm}}$$

$$Fe^{II} \xrightarrow{O_2} Fe^{II}O_2 \xrightarrow{e^-} Fe^{III}O_2^{2-} \underset{H_2O}{\overset{2H^+}{\xrightarrow{\hspace{1cm}} e^- \hspace{0.3cm}}} Fe^{IV}O^= \underset{}{\overset{H^+}{\xrightarrow{\hspace{0.5cm}} e^-}} Fe^{III}OH \underset{H_2O}{\overset{H^+}{\xrightarrow{\hspace{1cm}}}} Fe^{III}$$

with a downward e^- arrow from $Fe^{III}(cyt\ a_3)$ to Fe^{II}.

though the splitting of the O—O bond in $Fe^{III}O_2^{2-}$ may equally involve loss of water concerted with internal reduction to give a species like peroxidase compound I (p. 59) prior to further supply of electrons. One factor likely to contribute to the efficient reduction of O_2 without the release of peroxide or superoxide is that, after initial binding of O_2, cyt a_3 may remain locked in the more kinetically inert low-spin state (p. 31) until reaction is completed. The enzyme may also exhibit a 'capacitator' effect, storing two or more electrons (as Cu^I or cyt a^{II}) so that they can be delivered rapidly as soon as O_2 is bound.

4.4.2 The blue oxidases

These enzymes (laccase, ceruloplasmin and ascorbate oxidase) catalyse a number of one- and two-electron oxidations. In the oxidation of quinols by laccase, for instance, product semiquinones are thought to disproportionate non-enzymatically. O_2, however, is reduced directly to water in a four-electron reduction.

Laccase has been convincingly shown [19] to bind Cu in three different sites. The intense blue colour both of these enzymes and the blue electron carriers has been attributed to 'type-1' Cu in a distorted site (p. 35), which acts as an electron transfer group. Type-2 Cu is the so-called 'non-blue' Cu: its optical absorptions are overshadowed by those of type-1. It is accessible to small external ligands such as fluoride. Reduced laccase is fully oxidized by four oxidizing equivalents, but the resulting EPR signal accounts for only half the Cu^{II} atoms. The 'EPR-undetectable' (type-3) Cu is in the form of a pair of atoms 5–600 pm apart. In the cupric state they are characterized by an absorption at 330 nm, and their spins are coupled. The complement for laccase then is one type-1, one type-2 and two type-3 Cu atoms. Ascorbate oxidase has twice this total.

In laccase, it is supposed that O_2 is initially reduced to peroxide by a two-electron transfer from type-3 Cu_2^I, as in the formation of $HcnO_2$. Peroxide is then split and reduced to water in two further one-electron steps. Type-2 Cu binds one of the product water molecules, and also transfers electrons from type-1 to type-3 Cu. Type-1 Cu is the primary source of electrons, which it obtains by the oxidation of organic substrates.

Ceruloplasmin is thought to be important in Cu metabolism, and possibly catalyses the oxidation of Fe^{II} as it binds to transferrin [22]. *In vitro* it also catalyses the oxidation of amines such as adrenalin and serotonin. Its Cu chemistry is more complicated than that of laccase.

4.5 Oxygenases

These very widespread enzymes catalyse the insertion of O-atoms from O_2 into substrate molecules. Monoxygenases (hydroxylases, or mixed function oxidases) insert one O-atom into substrate and release the other as water. An obligatory second substrate supplies two electrons to reduce metal to a form in which it can activate O_2. Dioxygenases insert both O-atoms into substrate, often with the cleavage of a C—C bond. The oxygenase substrates for dioxygenases and some monoxygenases are often nucleophilic (electron-rich) phenolic compounds, which are themselves capable of reducing the catalytic metal. It is likely that such substrates may also bind to metal as an important feature of the reaction. (This occurs in quercetinase, an example of a Cu-containing dioxygenase.) Metals, however are not the only co-factors able to catalyse these reactions, as many monoxygenases are simple flavoproteins. Some typical oxygenases are shown in Table 4.5.

There are two principal mechanistic possibilities for metal-catalysed oxygenation, according to how the O_2 molecule is split. One is an oxene mechanism (see p. 31), in which, for Fe, a ferryl or $Fe^V O^{2-}$ intermediate reacts directly with substrate. The other involves the transfer of an activated $[O_2]$ species from metal to substrate: this is the most likely in dioxygenases. In the 'peracid' theory of cyt P450 action [27], for instance, peroxide is added to a neighbouring protein carboxylate group, losing oxide to give a peracid, which then attacks substrate:

$$Fe^{V}O^{=} + \bar{O}H + \bar{O}OC\text{-}R \longleftarrow [Fe^{III}O_2^{2-} + HOOC\text{-}R] \longrightarrow Fe^{III} + \bar{O}H + \bar{O}O\text{-}CO\text{-}R$$

(oxene route)   (peracid route)

Table 4.5 Molecular properties of some oxygenases

Enzyme	Mol wt	Co-factors
Monoxygenases		
Tyrosinase	$4 \times 32\,000$	4 Cu
Dopamine β-hydroxylase	$8 \times 36\,000$	4–7 Cu
Phenylalanine hydroxylase	$2 \times 50\,000$	2 Fe, pterin
Cytochrome P450	$40\,000$	1 haem *b*
Dioxygenases		
Protocatechuate 4,5 dioxygenase	$140\,000$	4 Fe
Protocatechuate 3,4 dioxygenase	$8 \times 87\,500$	8 Fe
L-tryptophan oxygenase	$4 \times 31\,000$	2 Cu, 2 haem *b*
Quercetinase	$110\,000$	2 Cu
Prolyl hydroxylase	$2 \times 65\,000$	Fe

4.5.1 Monoxygenases

The cytochromes P450 [27] are a remarkable group of haemoproteins, often involved in hydroxylating the more inert hydrocarbon groupings, for instance of bile acids, steroid hormones, drugs and fatty acids. They show properties both of cytochromes and of open-sided haem. In enzyme systems from *Pseudomonas putida*, electrons are supplied to P450 from NADH via a flavoprotein and the iron–sulphur protein putidaredoxin. P450 itself interacts with substrate and O_2. The reaction sequence in the camphor-hydroxylating system is as follows:

$$S \text{ (camphor)} \longrightarrow P450^{III}.S \xrightarrow{\;e^-\;} P450^{II}.S$$

$$P450^{III}$$

$$H_2O + SO \longleftarrow [P450^{II}O_2^{\cdot}.S] \xleftarrow{\;e^-\;} P450^{II}O_2.S \longleftarrow O_2$$

On binding substrate to $P450^{III}$ (the oxidized ferri-enzyme), a change from low to high-spin is observed, and one electron is taken up fairly quickly to give a high-spin Fe^{II} complex. This then rapidly takes up O_2 giving a compound resembling peroxidase compound III. The next step, which is rate-determining, is the acceptance of a second electron from putidaredoxin. The complex then rapidly decays to product (SO) and cyt $P450^{III}$. (For a comparison of this mechanism with that of peroxidase, see p. 59.) Systems isolated from adrenal mitochondria are similar, utilizing NADPH and adrenodoxin (which is homologous to putidaredoxin). Cyt P450 species may also comprise up to 20% of all protein in liver microsomes. These have a broader substrate specificity than those mentioned above, and obtain electrons from a pathway involving cyt b_5.

The spectrum of cyt P450 is unusual, and has been interpreted in terms of S(CYS) and N(HIS?) axial ligands to haem Fe. It is thought that CYS moves away on the binding of substrate to leave a system like myoglobin. It is clear that in all cyt P450 reactions, the flow of electrons, and the binding of substrate, are closely controlled so that reactive O_2 intermediates are only formed when substrate is in position for reaction.

Other types of monoxygenase are active in the metabolism of amino-acids. Consider, for instance the conversion of phenyl alanine to melanin, and to the neurogenic amines:

Phenylalanine hydroxylase (a) and tyrosine hydroxylase (b) in the catecholamine pathway are both pterin-requiring enzymes which utilize NADPH as a second substrate, and an enzymatic requirement for Fe has been demonstrated as well [51]. The latter enzyme is also stimulated *in vitro* by Ca^{2+} (p. 26).

Tyrosinase (polyphenol oxidase) is a Cu-enzyme which inserts an O-atom into a phenol. The product catechol can act as the second substrate for the reaction, in which it is further oxidized to a quinone:

Tyrosinase catalyses the conversion of tyrosine to melanin in several steps (b, c), including its hydroxylation and oxidation to dopaquinone. The lack of an EPR signal in the oxidized enzyme suggests that the Cu^{II} ions (presumably one per subunit, see Table 4.5) are grouped in spin-coupled pairs. As with haemocyanin, we can infer that the active site contains Cu_2 on a two-fold axis between subunits. We can summarize the reactions of the enzyme as follows:

The phenol and catechol need not be related: the fact that catechols enhance (but not allosterically) phenolase activity suggests that substrates for the two reactions are not bound at the same site. Since catechols can reduce the peroxy form of the enzyme, it follows that tyrosinase can act over-all as a catechol oxidase. The idea of a peroxide-like intermediate is supported by the finding that the Cu^{II} enzyme reacts with peroxide (dotted line) to give an intermediate resembling $HcnO_2$ in optical absorption. Its formation is slow, but it performs the phenolase reaction at physiological rates.

Dopamine β-hydroxylase, which follows later in the pathway of catecholamine oxidation (d), is a Cu-enzyme whose inorganic content has not been well defined. It requires ascorbate as a second substrate, and its mechanism of action can be interpreted as being similar to that of tyrosinase.

4.5.2 Dioxygenases

The catechuate dioxygenases are a group of enzymes which cleave the catechol ring. They vary in protein structure, but all contain labile non-haem, non-sulphur Fe. Those catalysing intradiol cleavage (a) are red, with high-spin Fe^{III}, while those catalysing extradiol cleavage (b or c) are colourless. The latter were originally thought to be Fe^{II} species, but Mossbauer and kinetic evidence can be interpreted, for protocatechuate 4,5 dioxygenase, in terms of two spin-paired Fe^{III} ions [74]. Fe–Fe spin-pairing interactions are also observed in the octameric protocatechuate 3,4 dioxygenase, on binding substrate. There is therefore the possibility that the Fe atoms in this group of enzymes, like those in haemerythrin, act in pairs to activate O_2.

Both the catechuate dioxygenases and L-tryptophan dioxygenase (reaction d) provide spectroscopic evidence of the participation of a ternary O_2-intermediate like peroxidase compound III, which forms only after the organic substrate has bound. The latter enzyme, and a possibly related enzyme with DL specificity, are of interest as they contain Cu with haem (like cytochrome oxidase), and they seem to use superoxide as a reaction intermediate.

The α-oxoglutarate oxygenases are a widely found group of enzymes which function as hydroxylases. One atom of O_2 is absorbed in hydroxylation of the substrate (DH_2), while the other is incorporated in a parallel obligatory oxidative decarboxylation of an oxo-acid:

$$O_2 + DH_2 + \text{R-CO-COOH} \longrightarrow \text{DHOH} + \text{R-COOH} + CO_2$$

The example of this type in Table 4.5 hydroxylates collagen proline in the sequence –X–PRO–GLY, and others include collagen lysine hydroxylase and γ-butyrobetaine hydroxylase. The enzymes require Fe and ascorbic acid, and contain active thiol groups.

4.6 Hydroperoxidases

These enzymes consume the biologically deleterious alkyl and hydrogen peroxides. Glutathione peroxidase destroys peroxides formed by the autoxidation of polyunsaturated fatty acids in membranes. (In endoplasmic reticulum, cyt P450 is also thought to perform this function.) Some peroxidases are adapted to oxidizing halide or thiocyanate ions for biosynthesis (thyroperoxidase in iodination, chloroperoxidase in fungal antibiotic elaboration), or for bacteriocidal action (lactoperoxidase in saliva, tears and milk, myeloperoxidase in granular leucocytes) ([47], cf. p. 48). While peroxides are reduced under the influence of peroxidases, they are disproportionated by catalase in a related reaction.

More than ten plant peroxidases have been found: turnip and radish both have a number ranging from the acidic (P_1) to the basic (P_7). The haem redox potentials are in the range $E'_0 = -300$ to $-150\,mV$, respectively. The resting ferric enzymes have spectra like Mb^{III}, suggesting an axial HIS co-ordination. (The low E'_0 of P_1, like that of catalase, ensures that no Fe^{II} is usually observed.) However, whereas Mb^{III} binds anions, the ferri-peroxidases bind an anion and a proton together. An acidic group near haem for proton binding would help explain the low redox potentials.

Table 4.6 Molecular properties of some hydroperoxidases

Enzyme	Mol wt	Co-factors
Plant peroxidases P_1-P_7	40 000	1 haem b
Cytochrome c peroxidase	34 100	1 haem b
Chloroperoxidase	42 000	1 haem b
Catalase	$4 \times (56 - 63\,000)$	4 haem b

Two catalytically active intermediates have been observed. Peroxidase initially combines with one peroxide molecule to give a green compound I, which is reduced by one electron from an organic substrate to give a pink compound II. Compound II has been established by Mossbauer spectroscopy as a ferryl (Fe^{IV}) species, and is reduced by a further electron to ferriperoxidase. (Two half-reduced organic substrates are then assumed to disproportionate spontaneously.) The structure of compound I is probably a ferryl haem with a porphyrin cation radical, or $Fe^V O^{2-}$. It contains only one of the O-atoms supplied by peroxide. A third complex of interest for comparison with other intermediates is compound III, formed *in vitro* from compound II with a large excess of H_2O_2. It is isomeric with MbO_2, but behaves rather more like a ferric superoxide or ferryl peroxide.

It is interesting to compare the reactions of haem in cyt P450 and peroxidase, as they may share common intermediates while performing different functions. The following hypothetical scheme [27] shows peroxidase activity on the left (loops A and B), and monoxygenase activity (oxene route) on the right (C and D):

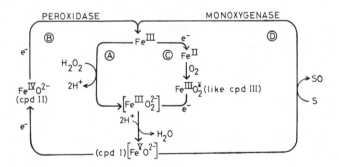

Both enzymes pass through Fe^{III} states, and both are thought to involve an intermediate of ferric peroxide type, which in peroxidase decays to compound I. The latter species go on to oxidize or oxygenate substrate (outer loops). The reactions of cyt P450 in which it utilizes peroxides, peracids or hypochlorite can be conceptually fitted to loops A and D of the scheme. Conversely, some peroxidases can act as monoxygenases (loops C and B). While Fe^{II} peroxidase species of lower E_o' (e.g. P_1) are rapidly autoxidized to Fe^{III}, P_7 and chloroperoxidase take up O_2 reversibly to give oxycomplexes with spectra suggestive of $Fe^{III}O_2^-$.

Cytochrome c peroxidase is induced in baker's yeast by O_2, and is an attractive enzyme for study. It is readily crystallized, with or without its haem b group, and the latter can be replaced by a Mn-porphyrin to give an enzyme of moderate activity. It combines very fast with peroxides to give a compound 'ES', which is stable in the absence of reductants. ES is similar in spectrum to compound II, but the EPR, in addition to the haem signal, shows a free radical band of equal intensity at $g = 2$, suggesting that one oxidizing equivalent has been transferred to a protein side-chain (see also p. 33). Two cyt c molecules reduce ES without observable intermediates.

Catalase activity is readily reproduced in simple compounds. Aqueous Fe^{III} at low pH, and ferrihaem at higher pH, disproportionate peroxide at rates varying with $[HO_2^-]$. Catalase itself has a pH-independent activity around neutrality, which approximates to that of the simpler species extrapolated to high pH. The significance of catalase and the peroxidases is that they can react with H_2O_2, the predominant species at physiological pH values, rather than with the anion HO_2^-. The first product of the catalase reaction is a green compound I, which decays with more peroxide to O_2, water and ferricatalase. In the presence of added reductants such as ethanol, peroxidase activity is shown, with the appearance of intermediates like compound II, and the dissociated catalase subunit shows loss of catalase activity and enhanced peroxidase activity. Catalase then seems to be a specialized peroxidase, capable of using the oxidative power of one peroxide molecule to oxidize another.

4.7 Some Oxygen-activating groups

O_2 is known to bind to three types of carrier protein, containing haem, Cu_2 and Fe_2 groups. (See p. 32 for a definition of the latter.) Table 4.7 shows that these groups also activate O_2 in a number of other proteins. It illustrates, first, a high degree of functional convergence between different protein types, and second, a versatility of role of the metal groups, subtly controlled and made specific within their protein

Table 4.7 The biological functions of some metal groupings

Normal function	Haem	Cu_2	Fe_2
O_2-carrier	Haemoglobin Myoglobin	Haemocyanin	Haemerythrin
4-e$^-$ oxidase	Cytochrome oxidase	Blue oxidases	—
Monoxygenase	Cytochrome P450	Tyrosinase	—
Dioxygenase	Tryptophan 2,3 dioxygenase	—	Catechuate oxygenases
Hydroperoxidase	Peroxidases Catalase	—	—

environments. We could amplify these points by adding other functions and other co-factors. Superoxide dismutases contain Cu/Zn, Fe or Mn; Mn is probably catalytic in the 'reverse oxidase' reaction of photosynthesis, and single Fe or Cu ions may catalyse some oxygenations. (Fe_2 also seems to be involved in some way in ribonucleotide reduction, p. 42). In fact, dioxygen species seem to be fairly non-specific in their catalytic metal requirements, and it is hard to believe that other proteins, with these or other transition metals, could not have evolved to perform many of the functions described in this chapter.

5 Metal metabolism

Metal metabolism consists of delivering the correct metal ion to act where it is needed. Uptake, transport, buffering, storage and excretion must ensure that physiologically necessary metals are made available, though not in excess, and that deleterious metals are excluded or rendered harmless. Enzymatic insertion is also sometimes necessary for adequate selectivity of binding of a metal at its active site. In this chapter we shall survey these metabolic processes before going on to discuss some aspects in more detail.

Adequate uptake of metals, whether from soil water, sea water, or the internalized environment of the animal gut, is the first requirement of metal metabolism. Free metal ions are hydrophilic and cannot readily diffuse across the lipid bilayer of the cell membrane. For this they require to be in fat-soluble compounds (e.g. haem), or to have carrier molecules which neutralize or conceal their charge, or to have access to hydrophilic channels through the membrane. Examples of carrier molecules include such products of animal digestion as sugars, amino-acids and small peptides. Some microbial ionophores are also carriers, while others are channel-formers. By such means metal ions may passively traverse membranes down their electrochemical gradients.

If a metal needs to be taken up against a concentration gradient, its transport across a membrane may be driven along with a one-way flux of a carrier molecule, or by coupling to the movement of another cation in the opposite direction (e.g. Ca^{2+}/Na^+ exchange). In addition, the major metals have specific enzymic ion-pumps, which couple metal transport to ATP hydrolysis. An alternative mechanism of uptake, pinocytosis, has been proposed for the uptake into the cell of vitamin B_{12} [15], and of the iron-carrier transferrin from plasma.

Many metals are taken up into the cell by mechanisms of relatively low metal affinity and specificity. The degree to which a metal present in the environment can be taken up is then determined in a complex fashion by competition with protons and other metals both for uptake sites on the cell surface and for extraneous ligands. (These interactions will be exemplified in the case of iron, p. 70). Metals which are taken up in excess, or are toxic, are then dealt with by more selective processes within the cell. However, both selectivity and efficiency of uptake are increased by the secretion of specific scavenging agents which bind metal ions and assist their absorption. These include microbial siderophores, and such gastro-intestinal secretions as intrinsic factor for Vitamin B_{12}, and a pancreatic factor for zinc.

Transport of metals from the gut lumen to the blood stream involves traversing mucosal epithelial cells and capillary endothelial cells. In general, where such transport across cells occurs, membranes must present differing activity towards metals at opposite faces of the cell to produce a net flux. Transport of the major metals, for instance, can be achieved by allowing passive diffusion at one cell face with active transport at the other, and a mechanism involving pinocytosis has also been proposed for calcium (p. 69). Various intracellular mucosal proteins appear to facilitate metal absorption from the gut in response to bodily requirements, including a Vitamin D induced Ca-binding protein and one resembling transferrin, but little is known of how they function.

Once metal ions have crossed the gut wall, they may appear in the plasma bound to small ligands, or else to specific transport proteins (Table 5.1). The latter circulate in the body fluids, reducing the activities and in some cases determining the destinations of the metals they carry. For instance, albumin carries copper principally from the gut to the liver, while carrying zinc principally from the liver to other tissues. Metals are retrieved from the body fluids by the same types of cellular uptake mechanisms as have already been mentioned, and can thus reach the various biological sites where they are needed.

However, control of metal ion concentrations is important, as even essential metals show toxic effects when present in excess. Major metals, for example, upset fluid balance or interfere with phosphate biochemistry, while minor metals promote oxygen toxicity or bind to active sulphydryl groups. A particular hazard, in the context of this chapter, is that metals compete for cation binding sites, and thus interfere with each other's functions. Homeostasis is achieved by active transport and storage mechanisms, and an additional factor in reducing free metal ion concentrations both within and without the cell is the buffering action of small molecules.

The major metal ions Ca^{2+} and Mg^{2+} are substantially buffered, while Na^+ and K^+ remain almost entirely free. Of the 2.5 mM Ca^{2+} in human plasma, half is bound to protein, 5% is chelated by small molecules such as citrate, and the rest is free. Of 0.7–0.9 mM Mg^{2+}, 25% is bound to large molecules. The levels of free Mg^{2+} are similar to those of Ca^{2+} in the extracellular fluids of diverse vertebrates [11]. Within the cell, accumulation of Ca^{2+} by cytoplasmic buffers or organelles can greatly increase the ratio of bound to free ion. In squid giant axon, for instance, $[Ca^{2+}]_i$ in a fresh preparation is 50 μM overall, but the concentration of free ion is only 30 nM. Some or all of the bound Ca^{2+} is in mitochondria near the cell membrane. Out of a total of around 10 mM Mg^{2+} in mammalian cells, only a small proportion is uncomplexed–estimates [54] have been made of 0.13 mM (rabbit skeletal muscle) and 0.1–1.9 mM (human erythrocytes). Mg^{2+} is mainly bound to ribosomes, nucleoside phosphates and other organic phosphates.

The minor metals are capable of competing both with the major metals and with each other for metal binding sites. Buffering by metabolites such as amino-acids is essential in reducing their free concentrations and limiting their toxic effects [2]. Thus even though the cellular content of iron approaches that of magnesium, and copper and zinc may both exceed calcium, these minor metals are almost entirely bound. Rabbit muscle phosphoglucomutase (PGM) binds Zn^{2+} a million times more strongly than Mg^{2+}, and the two metals do not differ greatly in overall concentration, yet 35–83% of PGM is found to be in the active Mg-form, rather than the inactive Zn-form (see also p. 24). Calculations from these data give a value of $10^{-10}M$ for free Zn^{2+} in the cytoplasm [50]. Again, although Cu^{2+}, among the divalent metals, shows the highest affinity for N and S ligands, its stereochemical preference for a square-planar co-ordination, together with the buffering action of small molecules, help to prevent it binding at inappropriate sites. For instance, carbonic anhydrase (and other Zn-enzymes) bind Cu^{2+} equally or more strongly than Zn^{2+} *in vitro*, a greater bond strength compensating for an unsuitable tetrahedral geometry (see Table 2.1). However, in the presence of equal concentrations of the two metals and an excess of free aminoacids (which can provide square planar co-ordination for Cu^{2+}), the enzyme binds $10^3 - 10^4$ times more Zn^{2+} than Cu^{2+} [2].

There are long-term reserves of some metals in the body, including cobalt (vitamin B_{12} in the liver), calcium (in bone) and iron. There is also a group of 'storage' molecules, including ferritin and metallothionein, which characteristically contain a high proportion of bound metal (Table 5.1). Physiologically, however, these molecules fulfill several functions, some quite unconnected with storing metals for future use. In the gut mucosa, which is continually shed and lost to the faeces, sequestering of dietary metals within the cell by these

Table 5.1 Metabolic proteins of the minor metals

Protein	Mol wt	Metal binding capacity
Transport proteins		
Transferrin	80 000	$2Fe^{III} + 2CO_3^{2-}$ (Zn from gut, ?Mn)
Ceruloplasmin	132 000	6–$7Cu^{II}$ (from liver)
Albumins	69 000	Cu^{II} from gut, Zn from liver, Ca, Ni
Transcobalamin II	38 000	Vitamin B_{12}
Nickeloplasmin	700 000	Ni^{II} (an α_1-macroglobulin)
Zn-protein	840 000	3–8Zn (from liver, an α_2-macroglobulin)
Storage proteins		
Ferritin	444 000	$4\,500Fe^{III}$ as $8FeOOH.FeO:OPO_3H_2$ (approx.)
Phosvitin	35 000	$47Fe^{III}$, green and brown forms
Metallothioneins	6 800	6–7M (= Zn,Cd,Cu,Hg,Ag,Bi) with 20 CYS
Cu-thionein	6 000	2.4Cu (human foetal liver)
Cu-thioneins	10 000	10,8,2 or 1Cu, with CYS:Cu = 2 : 1 (yeast)
Cu-proteins	10 000	Cu (liver, with varying CYS content)

molecules hinders their absorption. When such metals also enter the muscosal cells from the blood, a net excretion is even possible. In the liver and kidney, metallothionein and similar proteins bind copper and zinc, and probably serve as short-term reserves in controlling their supply to the body. Metallothioneins in gut and liver are also involved in dealing with extraneous toxic metals.

Lastly, if in spite of adequate metal supply, thermodynamic factors still do not favour the binding of an ion to its active site in the face of competition from other ions, this may be achieved by a specific ('chelatase') enzyme in a kinetically irreversible reaction. The formation of haem from Fe^{2+} and porphyrin for instance [26], although it can occur spontaneously, is catalysed by a ferrochelatase on the inner mitochondrial membrane. To return to zinc and magnesium, thermodynamic considerations suggest that chlorophyll should (like PGM) be largely contaminated with Zn^{2+}. The fact that it is not implies that Mg^{2+} is recognized by a chelatase which catalyses its rapid insertion into chlorophyll: this is then kinetically stable to substitution. A similar process probably ensures the purity of Co in cobalamin. All these insertions of metals into organic ring systems are highly selective.

Catalysed insertion belongs to a wider class of metal transformation reactions including redox manipulations of Co in the corrin ring system [68] and other metal ions. Microbes are responsible for the chemical alteration of many metals, including mercury, in the environment, by alkylation and dealkylation as well as redox reactions [64].

5.1 Microbial ion carriers
Many micro-organisms are capable of secreting secondary metabolites (p. 25) which either bind metal ions specifically, or facilitate their passage across cell membranes, or both. These 'ionophores' are important as antibiotics, but they have also found widespread biochemical applications in the study of cell processes depending on membrane transport, and as models for biological ion selectivity.

Although natural ionophores specific for some of the major metals have been found, it has not been shown that they play any part in normal metal metabolism. Rather, their role seems to be in 'chemical warfare', different species competing, in conditions of limited growth, by secreting ionophores to sabotage the ionic integrity of each other's membranes. Ionophores do play a direct part in the metabolism of iron. They are secreted by some bacterial species to chelate Fe^{III}, which is then taken up in its complexed form by an active process. These iron chelators are described separately under the heading 'siderophores', while a 'molybdophore' is mentioned on p. 75.

5.1.1 Ionophores
Ionophores [1] can mediate membrane transport either as channel-formers or as ion-carriers. The *channel-formers* amphotericin B and

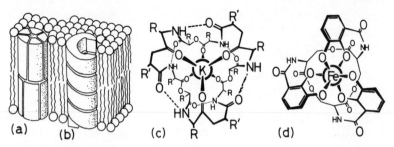

Fig. 5.1 Suggested molecular aggregates of (a) Amphotericin B and (b) Gramicidin A dissolved in a lipid bilayer may form pores with hydrophilic centre and hydrophobic surface. Ion-carrier complexes: (c) Valinomycin-K^+ and (d) Enterochelin-Fe^{3+}, with inward-pointing polar ligands and (c) outward pointing hydrophobic side-chains, $R(-CH(CH_3)_2)$ and $R'(-CH_3)$. Each of the metals is octahedrally co-ordinated.

nystatin are synthesized by *Streptomyces* species, and have a lytic effect on fungi. Amphotericin B is a polyhydroxylic lactone which can span half the thickness of a lipid bilayer. About ten molecules are thought to assemble to surround a water-filled channel of 0.5 nm diameter (Fig. 5.1a). Non-polar groups in the molecule interact with cholesterol in the membrane. These large pores allow the passage of urea, glycol, glycerol and hydrated metal ions. However, they are partially selective to anions (e.g. Cl^- over Na^+), and exclude sucrose. Gramicidin A is a linear polypeptide which can, it is proposed, form a helix of 6.3 residues per turn. Two such helices span a membrane end-to-end, with a 0.4 nm diameter channel down the centre (Fig. 5.1b). The channel is too small to pass fully hydrated cations, and carbonyl groups forming the channel wall are required to move so that their oxygen atoms co-ordinate metal ions in transit. The structural distortion this causes, greatest for a small cation, is probably responsible for the ion selectivity $NH_4^+ > K^+ > Na^+$.

The *ion-carrier* molecules (mol wt 200–2000), which themselves carry ions through the membrane, have non-polar exteriors and polar interiors. Many are neutral macrocycles like valinomycin, while others, like nigericin and monensin, are linear polyethers which form H-bonded rings around a metal ion.

Valinomycin is a cyclic dodecadepsipeptide with a high selectivity for K^+ over Na^+ and other alkali metal ions. In its K^+ complex (Fig. 5.1c), six ester carbonyl oxygen atoms are approximately octahedrally co-ordinated to the metal ion, and the molecule forms an enclosing bracelet held rigidly by H-bonds. It is thought that a smooth conformation change allows the metal to be released as the ligand adopts its flatter, more open, uncomplexed form. Two factors determine selectivity in this case: the free energies of complex formation and of hydration of the various metals. The former reflect the flexibility of the ligand and the bond strength and snugness of fit with the ion, while the latter, for the alkali metals, are in reverse order to their ionic radii (Table 2.2, p. 16). Selection of K^+ over Na^+ may be largely due to the greater hydration energy of Na^+.

5.1.2 Siderophores

Bacterial iron-chelating agents are usually hydroxamic acid derivatives or polyhydric phenols, and have a high enough affinity for Fe^{III} to mobilize it from its insoluble hydroxide at pH 7. The synthesis of such ligands is stimulated in conditions of iron deprivation, and the iron chelate is then taken up by the organism. Such chelation of course actually reduces the chemical activity of the metal, and once inside the cell, a further input of energy is required to release the free ion from the complex.

Two independant Fe-transport systems have been demonstrated in *E. coli*. In the presence of 1 mM citrate, an Fe-uptake system with a K_m for iron of about $0.2 \mu M$ is induced rapidly. Possibly citrate acts as a carrier molecule. A second system involves the synthesis of enterochelin (enterobactin), a cyclic triester of *L*-SER with three dihydroxybenzoate residues attached by amide bonds (Fig. 5.1d). Iron is transported into the cell as Fe^{III}-enterochelin. Further utilization of the ion requires rapid hydrolytic cleavage of the ligand within the cell to dihydroxybenzoyl-N-serine (DBS), and Fe^{III} can then be reduced as its DBS complex. DBS cannot be reused in the synthesis of enterochelin, and is released from the cell. The esterase activity, and the synthesis of enterochelin, is repressed by iron in the culture medium at 5 mM concentration, although in iron-rich media large amounts of iron may be accumulated.

5.2 The major metals

5.2.1 Translocation across membranes

The movements of the major metal ions across membranes can never be separated from those of protons and anions: there is a complex relationship between pH, transmembrane electrical potential, and the various concentration differences. To illustrate these relationships, we shall consider a few of the many active ion transport systems which have been described.

There is universal need to expel Na^+ from the cell and to accumulate K^+. Animals, and plants to a certain degree, depend on a membrane ATPase which exchanges Na^+ for K^+. Procaryotes, on the other hand, have a system which links ATP hydrolysis (or oxidative phosphorylation) to proton translocation. The resulting proton electrochemical gradient provides the motive power for many other transport processes, including Na^+ expulsion.

The Na/K-activated ATPase of most higher organisms (Fig. 2.2) expels 3 Na^+ from the cell with the consumption of 1 ATP and the influx of 1–2 K^+. In the cycle of reaction (which requires Mg^{2+}) ATP and Na^+ bind on the inner surface of the membrane and ATP transfers a phosphoryl group to an active ASP residue with a simultaneous enzyme conformation change. Na^+ is expelled at the outer surface, and K^+ is bound. The aspartyl phosphate is hydrolysed and the conformation change is reversed with the release of K^+ on the inner surface. Two protein subunits have been identified. One (mol wt 50 000) is a glycoprotein, while the other (mol wt 95 000) contains the active ASP residue.

In *Streptococcus faecalis*, the expulsion of Na^+ and H^+ in exchange for K^+ at the cell membrane is linked to the hydrolysis of ATP. K^+ can be concentrated by a factor of 2000. A simple model [28] involves three distinct systems. First, an electrogenic ATPase expels protons, setting up both a pH and an electrical potential gradient. Second, Na^+ is expelled in exchange for H^+. Since there is no net charge transfer involved, this exchange must be driven by the proton concentration gradient. It can work against a ten to twenty-fold Na^+ concentration gradient. Last, there is a K^+ influx which seems to be electrophoretic, i.e. K^+ is moved against its concentration gradient by the voltage difference across the membrane. However, K^+ does not escape when the voltage gradient is dissipated by a decrease in ATP supply to the ATPase. It is therefore proposed that the diffusion of K^+ across the membrane is 'gated', in that it takes place only when the potential difference is adequate to ensure accumulation. Otherwise the membrane becomes impermeable. (cf. the voltage-dependent Na^+-channels mentioned on p. 26.)

Many cellular processes depend on $[Ca^{2+}]_i$ being kept very low. A Na^+/Ca^{2+} exchange pump, which uses the normal Na^+ concentration gradient across the plasma membrane to expel Ca^{2+}, is thought to operate in nerve, muscle of all types, and gut. If one assumes an exchange of at least $3 Na^+$ for $1 Ca^{2+}$, then $[Ca^{2+}]_i$ may theoretically be reduced to 0.1 μM. Muscle cells, however, also utilize large internal supplies of Ca^{2+} (Chapter 2), which are stored either in sarcoplasmic reticulum or in mitochondria, each of which has its own uptake mechanism. The Ca/Mg-activated ATPase of sarcoplasmic reticulum, for instance (Table 2.4, p. 28), is adequate to reduce $[Ca^{2+}]_i$ to 0.07–0.1 μM in crustacean muscle. (Similar enzyme systems are also found in erythrocyte membrane and other non-excitable tissue. Ca^{2+} within the sarcoplasmic reticulum is buffered by calsequestrin and a high-affinity protein (Table 2.4).

Mitochondrial Ca^{2+} uptake may be driven either by ATP hydrolysis or electron transport. It also involves a high affinity site ($K_D \sim 1 \mu$M). We have already noted a possible influence of Ca^{2+} on mitochondrial enzyme function (p. 27). Normal reversible Ca^{2+} uptake ('membrane loading') is coupled to proton release. In other circumstances, Ca^{2+} may be taken up together with a permeant anion such as phosphate. It is bound relatively irreversibly, in quantities up to 3μmol Ca/mg protein, and deposits of calcium salts appear. Such 'matrix loading' occurs in cells actively concerned with calcium metabolism such as osteoblasts, osteoclasts, calcifying chondrocytes, and cells of egg-shell glands. It occurs early in many pathological conditions, probably because of increased influx across the plasma membrane. If excessive, it leads to loss of mitochondrial function.

5.2.2 The internal fluid media of animals

Fifty years ago, it was noted that the ratios of cation concentrations in the extracellular fluids (blood, haemolymph etc.) of different animals were similar to those of seawater, and it was proposed that these composition ratios had become fixed at the time when marine creatures first enclosed internal fluid media (see Table 1.2). Although this evolutionary theory must be rejected in favour of more direct considerations of cell requirements [11], the similarities are there, between marine creatures with $[Na^+]_i$ greater than the concentration in seawater (470 mM), and freshwater animals with values of less than 50 mM. The advantage in evolutionary terms for non-marine animals to dilute their plasma is that less energy is required in maintaining chemical gradients. A large number of terrestrial mammals, birds and reptiles hold $[Na^+]_e$ at around 160 mM, enabling a similar $[K^+]_i$ to be maintained in excitable tissue. We have already noted that this seems to be an optimum value for muscle.

The most striking similarity between the extracellular fluids and seawater is the constancy of the ratio Na/K. As a general trend, this can be related to the requirements of nervous tissue. If $[Na^+]_e/[K^+]_e$, and p_{Na}/p_K (membrane permeabilities) are kept constant, and $[Na^+]_i \approx [K^+]_i$, then a constant optimal trans-membrane potential results. Model calculations along these lines have been made relating overall potential to ionic balance. Diffusible Ca^{2+} is also found to vary with alkali ion concentrations in vertebrates in a way which can be related to membrane requirements.

The fastidious requirements of excitable membrane implied by these relationships is matched by precise homeostatic control over internal electrolyte concentrations. Alkali metal ion levels in extra-cellular fluids are adjusted by the effect of thirst and salt craving on intake, and the influence of antidiuretic hormone and aldosterone on reabsorption in the kidney tubules. To achieve this fine control the human kidneys, for instance, filter the entire plasma volume about every 20 min.

The homeostasis of calcium in humans is regulated physiologically by the hormones calcitonin and parathyroid hormone, and the active metabolites of vitamin D_3. In terms of transport mechanisms it presents a special problem, as the close regulation of millimolar plasma concentrations involves large fluxes across gut, kidney and bone epithelia which themselves must limit cytoplasmic Ca^{2+} to micromolar levels. Recent experiments with chick small intestine and chorioallantoic membrane preparations indicate that intracellular Ca^{2+} is sequestered in vesicles [12]. It is thought that pinocytosis at one cell face produces cytoplasmic vesicles containing extracellular fluid (Na^+ and $1\,mM$ Ca^{2+}). The normal membrane calcium pump now loads the vesicle with Ca^{2+} from the cytoplasm in exchange for Na^+, and the Ca^{2+}-rich vesicles are eventually discharged on the opposite face of the cell.

5.3 The minor metals
Some of the compounds involved in the metabolism of the minor metals were shown in Table 5.1. It is appropriate to mention here a group of small (mol wt 6000–12 000) cysteine-rich proteins which have been isolated from various animal tissues [36]. Their synthesis is induced in the presence of metal ions, and they seem to act in detoxification. They are also important in the metabolism of Cu and Zn, acting as storage buffers, and possibly in transport processes. The different proteins apparently vary in metal and CYS content, and the metal content of any one protein may depend on the tissue from which it is prepared. Cu-binding proteins have also been found in yeast.

Metallothioneins (mol wt 6800) are among the smallest of the group. They are abundant in liver and kidney parenchyma, and in intestine, and their biosynthesis is induced by Zn, Cu, Cd, Hg, Ag and Bi. (The last four metals have no known physiological function.) A horse and a human protein are homologous in 55 out of 61 residues, including 20 CYS (with no disulphide bonds). Each binds seven metal atoms: 7Zn (human) and 4.6Cd + 2.5Zn (equine), together with traces of Cu. It is possible from the stoichiometry that each metal binding site is formed by 2–3 CYS ligands: the chain contains seven –CYS–X–CYS– sequences.

5.3.1 *Iron*
Iron is the most abundant minor metal in humans, totalling 3–4 g in an adult. About two thirds of this circulates as haemoglobin, one tenth is in myoglobin, and less than 1% is in transferrin and all iron enzymes and redox proteins. The remainder comprises the iron stores ferritin and haemosiderin, found principally in liver, spleen and bone marrow.

A small daily intake of iron is needed to replace average daily losses in faeces and urine (1 mg). menstruation (0.6–1.2 mg) and pregnancy (1.6 mg). The proportion of dietary iron absorbed is raised in iron deficiency and states associated with increased erythropoiesis. In these circumstances a transferrin-like substance is found in mucosal cells. When dietary iron is excessive, it accumulates in mucosal ferritin, partially circumventing its absorption.

Many other factors affect the uptake of iron. Fe^{III} in the diet must be dissolved and (possibly) reduced before it can be absorbed. Gastric acid temporarily disperses Fe^{III} so that it can be bound in small complexes. (Iron is absorbed mainly from the human jejunum.) Ascorbic acid enhances the uptake of Fe^{III}, reducing and solubilizing it, and also of Fe^{II}, which it may chelate. However, powerful iron chelators such as EDTA or desferrioxamine, or a large excess of ascorbic acid, depress the uptake of iron by competing with uptake sites for the metal.

The poor uptake of iron from vegetable sources (1–7% absorbed) arises from the presence of oxalate, phosphate and especially phytic acid (inositol hexaphosphate), which bind iron. Ca^{2+} enhances the uptake of iron in small amounts (by competing for phosphates) but depresses it in large amounts (by competing for uptake sites.) Iron from animal sources is better absorbed (11–22%). This partly reflects a higher content of haem, which is absorbed unchanged, and fewer insolubilizing ligands. In addition, peptides and amino acids from protein digestion facilitate the uptake of non-haem iron, even from vegetable material in the diet.

Transferrin (Tfn) is the β-globulin responsible for the transport of iron between animal tissues. It takes up iron released into the blood stream from the gut mucosa, from storage, and from haem catabolism in the reticuloendothelial system. It has been proposed that the uptake of iron by Tfn involves the oxidation of Fe^{II}, and that this is catalysed by the plasma Cu-protein ceruloplasmin [22]. This could partly explain how Cu-deficiency in animals, by disrupting Fe-metabolism, causes anaemia. Tfn delivers iron to bone marrow, iron stores and other tissues, and may also be involved in the transport of Zn and Mn. In humans, 30–35 mg of Fe released in the breakdown of haem is recycled daily via Tfn to erythroblasts in the bone marrow.

Tfn is a glycoprotein with two similar Fe-binding sites (Table 5.1), and the sequences of the N-terminal and C-terminal halves of the molecule, each containing one site, reveal strong (about 40%) homology. Fe^{III} is bound with great avidity. Under physiological conditions the estimated apparent dissociation constant ($k_D \equiv [Tfn][Fe^{III}]/[Tfn.Fe^{III}]$) is 10^{-24} M. The protein probably provides 2–3 TYR and 1–2 HIS ligands to iron at each site. Further metal co-ordination sites may be filled by CO_3^{2-} (H-bonded to a more distant basic residue) and water. The two sites are very slightly different in their binding and kinetic properties.

Human Tfn accounts for about 0.1% of body iron. The protein is normally 30% saturated. Iron exerts a negative feedback effect on the biosynthesis of Tfn, so that in iron deficiency more protein circulates (higher total iron binding capacity) with a reduced relative and absolute iron content. Tfn is a true carrier of half life ten days. Its iron content turns over ten times every day. It is thought to bind to specific receptor proteins on the surface of target cells, and is probably taken up by pinocytosis. It is then released in the extracellular fluid again when its iron has been removed.

Tfn is related to the proteins ovalbumin (from avian egg yolk) and lactoferrin (from milk and other secretions). All three proteins are of similar size, have sequence homologies, and bind two Fe^{III} very strongly. They probably share a bacteriostatic function in reducing free iron to a very low level.

Ferritin [30] is a protein with a large capacity for storing iron (Table 5.1), found in animals, plants, and possibly also bacteria [63]. It acts as a temporary store preventing toxic build-up of iron concentration, and as a long-term mobilizable reserve. The iron is in the form of a hydrous ferric oxide–phosphate complex. A protein shell (apoferritin) surrounds micelles of the inorganic complex, thus rendering the Fe^{III} soluble in the cytoplasm. Apoferritin biosynthesis is stimulated at the level of translation by the presence of free Fe, and there is usually an overproduction of protein so that a reserve capacity for iron is created.

The X-ray structure of horse-spleen apoferritin [7] shows a compact, fairly smooth protein shell of internal and external diameter 7.5 and 13.0 nm, respectively. The 24 subunits are arranged with cubic (4 3 2) symmetry, and six channels penetrate the shell at the four-fold axes (Fig. 5.2). Cation binding sites are found both on the inner and outer surfaces: some of the former may reasonably be involved in iron binding and accumulation. The inorganic micelle, which contributes up to 50% by weight of ferritin, consists of one or more microcrystals, whose orientation is not related to that of the protein shell.

The oxidation of Fe^{II} *in vitro* under a variety of conditions is catalysed by apoferritin, all the resultant Fe^{III} being found within partly filled ferritin molecules. The kinetics are complex and the detailed mechanism controversial. One model involves the chelation of Fe^{II} at sites on the inner surface of apoferritin, with carboxyl and possibly HIS ligands, which promote its autoxidation. The resultant bound Fe^{III} form nuclei of 'FeOOH' crystallites in a slow phase of reaction, and the reaction speeds up as the crystallites grow and surface catalytic sites appear to which Fe^{II} as well as Fe^{III} can bind. The formation of ferritin *in vivo* almost certainly involves the incorporation of iron into preformed apoferritin, but an oxidative mechanism has not been established.

Ferritin iron can be removed by the action of a number of reducing agents including thioglycollic acid, cysteine, ascorbic acid and

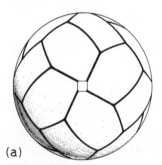
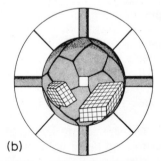

Fig. 5.2 *Ferritin.* (a) Spherical shell model, viewed down a channel (four-fold axis), showing proposed domains of the protein subunits. (b) Model cut away to show further channels, and two microcrystals within the shell.

reduced riboflavin. An NADH-FMN oxidoreductase isolated from liver may represent a biological ferritin reductase, supplying $FMNH_2$ to convert Fe^{III} to Fe^{II}. Ferritin is also degraded in lysosomes. Here the protein shell is partly or completely digested, leaving a microcrystalline residue of similar composition to ferritin micelles with some adhering protein material. This substance, *haemosiderin*, is the second principal form of storage iron found in animals. Mobilization of iron in this case also may involve a reducing agent.

In iron loss or deficiency, the first call is on a small labile pool of iron in equilibrium with ferritin and haemosiderin. This pool probably consists of small complexes in transit between stores, cell membranes and mitochondria. The stores then become depleted, and iron absorptivity in the gut increases. (This is the only site of control of iron balance.) As the stores disappear, transferrin concentration and saturation change (see above) and anaemia develops.

Iron overload due to excessive intake or repeated transfusion leads to a widespread laying down of storage iron. Ferritin and haemosiderin appear in many tissues, where eventual damage occurs. It is surprising that for such an important metal there is no natural method of excretion.

Phosvitin is an interesting iron storage molecule of unknown function obtained from avian egg yolk (Table 5.1). It is a phosphoglycoprotein containing many phosphoserine residues arranged mainly in continuous clusters of up to eight in length. In the presence of oxygen and phosvitin, Fe^{II} is rapidly oxidized to a bound form of Fe^{III} with accompanying release of inorganic phosphate, two phosphate groups remaining for every iron bound. Magnetic and spectroscopic studies [69] on the green complex indicate that Fe^{III} is tetrahedrally co-ordinated by phosphate oxygen atoms. Phosphate bridging, with sharing of tetrahedral edges, probably results in linear arrays of magnetically interacting Fe ions.

5.3.2 Zinc

Zinc is nearly as abundant in the human body as iron, totalling $1-2\,g$ in adults. Its absorption from the gut is enhanced by a low molecular weight factor found in human (but not bovine) milk, and pancreatic secretions, probably prostaglandin E_2. After absorption, zinc is probably carried in the portal blood bound to transferrin. In the liver it is transferred to other circulating proteins, mainly albumin, but also to an α_2-macroglobulin (Table 5.1).

The uptake of zinc by gut mucosa varies inversely with the amount of mucosal metallothionein present. The latter, in turn, is increased in response to increased deposition of zinc in mucosal cells from the blood. Mucosal metallothionein therefore controls zinc absorption in response to plasma zinc status by sequestering zinc in the mucosa. Metallothionein in hepatocytes is also utilized for temporary storage or detoxification of zinc, so that in both liver and intestine, this protein is a key ligand in maintaining homeostasis. Zinc is lost from the body by deposition in mucosal cells and desquamation into the faeces as Zn-metallothionein.

5.3.3 Copper

Copper absorption from the gut takes place in the stomach or upper small intestine, probably by means of small peptide or amino-acid complexes. Copper not immediately transported to the portal circulation becomes bound to a mucosal metallothionein-like protein, which is induced by high levels of dietary copper, and serves to divert some of the absorbed copper back into the faeces as the mucosa is desquamated. Some copper is also incorporated directly into superoxide dismutase in the duodenal mucosa.

As copper emerges into the portal plasma, it binds to albumin in equilibrium with ionic Cu^{II} and a small pool of amino acid complexes. This system allows copper to be absorbed and accumulated in the liver. It is then excreted in the bile, or incorporated into ceruloplasmin and returned to the blood. The liver and gut together thus control copper homeostasis, since little plasma copper is dialysable or susceptible to glomerular filtration.

The copper in ceruloplasmin, which normally constitutes 95% of plasma copper, is firmly bound and not readily exchangeable. As a result, uptake of copper by extrahepatic tissues, which seems to depend on ceruloplasmin transport [22], may necessitate degradation or conformational change in the carrier protein. Alternatively, it is possible that *in vivo* as *in vitro* with many Cu-proteins, the incorporation or exchange of copper atoms requires reduction to Cu^{I}.

About half the normal hepatic copper is bound by cytoplasmic proteins, and up to 20% appears in the nuclear fraction, where it may be involved in a structural role with polynucleotides. 20% is in the mitochondrial–lysosomal fraction, and accumulation by lysosomes may represent the route to biliary excretion. The remainder is in the microsomal fraction, probably in the course of ceruloplasmin synthesis. The cytoplasmic Cu-proteins are several and include a metallothionein, and two proteins containing aromatic residues and 15% and 5%, respectively, of cysteine. The synthesis of these is induced at the level of transcription by increased Cu. Synthesis of apoceruloplasmin is also stimulated, in adult mammals, though its level does not drop in copper deficiency. The liver can thus get rid of copper by using ceruloplasmin as a long-term buffer, as well as by biliary excretion. In neonate rats (with a low capacity for ceruloplasmin synthesis), copper injection led to elevated hepatic levels for nearly 2 weeks, while adult rats could transfer all excess copper from liver to plasma in 3 days.

In the bile, copper is initially complexed with amino and bile acids, but as it proceeds it becomes strongly bound, probably to conjugated bilirubin. This binding prevents the reabsorption of the metal from the gall bladder.

5.3.4 Other metals

We have mentioned in passing Co (as vitamin B_{12}), Mn, Mo and Ni, as well as Hg and Cd. Mo, available as the anion MoO_4^{2-}, is likely to be taken up by similar routes to SO_4^{2-} and HPO_4^{2-}. A Mo-binding ionophore has been described [33]. This is a peptide of mol wt 550 which binds MoO_4^{2-} to give a bright yellow complex. The ionophore is secreted by *Bacillus thuringiensis* in conditions of iron depletion: its biological significance is unknown.

Suggestions for further reading

A. Monographs on related subjects

Phipps, D. A. (1976), *Metals and Metabolism*, Oxford University Press. Complementary to this text in its treatment of relevant inorganic chemistry, and terrestrial distribution, of the biological metals.

Simkiss, K. (1975), *Bone and Biomineralisation*, Edward Arnold, London. Readable short account, in terms of how science actually progresses.

Calvin, M. (1969), *Chemical Evolution*, Oxford University Press. Describes classic experiments in simulating primeval chemical reactions.

Jones, C. W. (1975), *Biological Energy Conservation*, Chapman and Hall, London (this series). Useful background to electron transport.

B. Comprehensive reference texts, with the chapters which they cover

Eichhorn, G. L. (ed) (1974), *Inorganic Biochemistry*, vols. I and II, Elsevier, Amsterdam. For chapters 2–5.

Hayaishi, O. (ed) (1974), *Molecular Mechanisms of Oxygen Activation*, Academic Press, New York. For Chapter 4 (except oxygen carriers).

Hoekstra, W. G., Suttie, J. W., *et al.* (eds) (1974), *Trace Element Metabolism in Animals—II*, University Park Press, Baltimore. For Chapters 1 and 5.

Jacobs, A. and Worwood, M. (eds) (1974), *Iron in Biochemistry and Medicine*, Academic Press, New York. For Chapters 3–5.

Lovenberg, W. (ed) (1973, 1977), *Iron-sulfur Proteins*, vols. I–III, Academic Press, New York. For chapters 3 and 4.

Neilands, J. B. (ed) (1974), *Microbial Iron Metabolism*, Academic Press, New York. For Chapter 5.

Ponnamperuma, C. (ed) (1977), *Chemical Evolution of the Early Precambrian*, Academic Press, New York. For Chapter 1.

Sigel, H. (ed) (1973–7), *Metal Ions in Biological Systems*, vols. I–VII, Marcel Dekker, New York. For Chapters 2–5.

Wasserman, R. H. (ed) (1977), *Calcium-binding Proteins and Calcium Function*, Elsevier, Amsterdam. For Chapters 2 and 5

C. More selective texts, to which reference is made for the sake of particular chapters of interest

[1]   Addison, A. W., Cullen, W. R., Dolphin, D. and James, B. R. (eds) (1977), *Biological Aspects of Inorganic Chemistry*, John Wiley, New York.

[2]   Williams, D. R. (ed) (1976), *An Introduction to Bio-Inorganic Chemistry*, C. C. Thomas, Springfield, Illinois.

[3]   Williams, R. J. P. and da Silva, J. R. R. F. (eds) (1978), *New Trends in Bio-Inorganic Chemistry*, Academic Press, New York.

D. Detailed references

[4]   Adman, E. T. Stenkamp, R. E., *et al.* (1978), *J. mol. Biol.*, **123**, 35–48.

[5]   Argos, P. and Matthews, F. S. (1975), *J. biol. Chem.*, **250**, 747–51.

[6]   Babior, B., Curnutte, J. T., *et al.* (1975), *J. Lab. clin. Med.*, **85**, 235–44.
[7]   Banyard, S. H., Stammers, D. K., *et al.* (1978), *Nature*, **271**, 282–84.
[8]   Bennett, L. E. (1973), *Prog. inorg. Chem.*, **18**, 1–176.
[9]   Brewer, G. J. and Eaton, J. W. (1971), *Science*, **171**, 1205–22.
[10]   Bridgen, J. M., Harris, J. I. *et al.* (1975), *FEBS Letts.*, **49**, 392–95.
[11]   Burton, R. F. (1973), *Biol. Revs.*, **48**, 195–231.
[12]   Carafoli, E. and Crompton, M. (1978), *Current Topics in Membranes and Transport*, **10**, 151–216.
[13]   Chock, P. B. and Titus, E. O. (1973), *Prog. inorg. Chem.*, **18**, 287–382.
[14]   Colman, P. M. (1977), *Proc. 4th. Int. Cong. Photosynthesis*, 810–13.
[15]   DiGirolamo, P. M. and Huennekens, F. M. (1975), *Arch. Biochem. Biophys.*, **168**, 386–93.
[16]   Dixon, N. E., Gazzola, C., *et al.* (1976), *Science*, **191**, 1144–50.
[17]   Dunn, M. F. (1975), *Structure and Bonding*, **23**, 61–122.
[18]   Eisenberger, P., Shulman, R. G. *et al.* (1978), *Nature*, **274**, 30–4.
[19]   Fee, J. A. (1975), *Structure and Bonding*, **23**, 1–60.
[20]   Fenna, R. E. and Matthews, B. W. (1975), *Nature*, **258**, 573–7.
[21]   Frieden, E. (1974), *Adv. exptl. med. Biol.*, **48**, 1–32.
[22]   Frieden, E. and Hsieh, H. S. (1976), *Adv. Enzym.*, **44**, 187–236.
[23]   Frenkel, A. W. (1970), *Biol. Revs.*, **45**, 569–616.
[24]   Gabel, N. W. (1977), *Prog. molec. and subcell. Biol.*, **5**, 145–72.
[25]   Glusker, J. P. (1971), *The Enzymes* **V**, 413–39.
[26]   Granick, S. and Beale, S. I. (1978), *Adv. Enzym.*, **46**, 33–203.
[27]   Gunsalus, I. C. and Sligar, S. G. (1978), *Adv. Enzym.*, **47**, 1–44.
[28]   Harold, F. M. and Altendorf, K. (1974), *Current Topics in Membranes and Transport*, **5**, 1–50.
[30]   Harrison, P. M. (1977), *Seminars in Haematology*, **14**, 55–70.
[31]   Haugaard, N. (1968), *Physiol. Revs.*, **48**, 311–73.
[32]   Hogenkamp, H. P. C. and Sando, G. N. (1974), *Structure and Bonding*, **20**, 23–58.
[33]   Ketchum, P. A. and Owens, M. S. (1975), *J. Bact.*, **122**, 412–17.
[34]   Klotz, I. M., Klippenstein, G. L., *et al.* (1976), *Science*, **192**, 335–44.
[35]   Knowles, P. F., Marsh, D. and Rattle, H. W. E. (1976), *Magnetic Resonance of Biomolecules*, John Wiley, New York.
[36]   Kojima, Y. and Kagi, J. H. R. (1978), *Trends Biol. Sci.*, **3**, 90–3.
[37]   Kretsinger, R. H. (1976), *Ann. Revs. Biochem.*, **45**, 239–66.
[38]   Larsen, H. (1967), *Adv. microbial Physiol.*, **1**, 97–132.
[39]   Macara, I. G., McLeod, G. C., *et al.* (1979), *Biochem. J.*, **181**, 457–65.
[40]   McDonald, C. C., Phillips, W. D., *et al.*, (1974), Biochemistry, **13**, 1952–9.
[41]   MacDonald, M. J. Bentle, L. A., *et al.* (1978), *J. Biol. Chem.*, **253**, 116–24.
[42]   Margulis, L. (1974), *Evolutionary Biology*, **7**, 45–78.
[43]   Mildvan, A. S. and Grisham, C. M., (1974), *Structure and Bonding*, **20**, 1–21.
[44]   Moore, G. and Williams, R. (1976), *Coord. Chem. Revs.*, **18**, 125–97.
[45]   Morgenroth, V., Boadle-Biber, M., *et al.* (1974), *P. N. A. S.*, **71**, 4283–7.
[46]   Morris, J. G. (1975), *Adv. microbial Physiol.*, **12**, 169–246.
[47]   Morrison, M., Schonbaum, G. R., *et al.* (1976), *Ann. Revs. Biochem.*, **45**, 861–88.
[48]   O'Brien, R. W. (1975), *J. Bact.*, **122**, 468–73.
[49]   Odutuga, A. A., Prout, R. E. S., *et al.* (1975), *Arch. Oral Biol.*, **20**, 311–16.
[50]   Peck, E. J. and Ray, W. R. (1971), *J. biol. Chem.*, **246**, 1160–7.

[51]   Petrack, B., Sheppy, F., *et al.* (1972), *J. biol. Chem.*, **247**, 4872-8.
[52]   Phillips, S. E. V. (1978), *Nature*, **273**, 247-8.
[53]   Pocker, Y. and Sarkanen, S. (1978), *Adv. Enzym.*, **47**, 149-274.
[54]   Purich, D. L., Fromm, H. J., *et al.* (1973), *Adv. Enzym.*, **39**, 249-326.
[55]   Rasmussen, H. and Goodman, D. B. P. (1975), *Ann. N. Y. Acad. Sci.*, **253**, 789-96.
[56]   Reuter, H. (1973), *Prog. biophys. and mol. Biol.*, **26**, 1-43.
[57]   Richardson, J. S., Thomas, K. A., *et al.* (1975), *P. N. A. S.*, **72**, 1349-53.
[58]   Rubin, A. H., Terasaki, M. *et al.* (1978), *P. N. A. S.*, **75**, 2879-83.
[59]   Ryden, L. and Lundgren, J-O. (1976), *Nature*, **261**, 344-46.
[60]   Salemme, F. R. (1977), *Ann. Revs. Biochem.*, **46**, 299-329.
[61]   da Silva, J. J. R. F. and Williams, R. J. P. (1976), *Structure and Bonding*, **29**, 67-121.
[62]   Smellie, R. M. S. (1974), *Biochem. Soc. Symp.* no. **39**.
[63]   Stiefel, E. I. and Watt, G. D. (1979), *Nature*, **279**, 81-3.
[64]   Summers, A. and Silver, S. (1978), *Ann. Rev. Microb.*, **32**, 637-72.
[65]   Taborsky, G. (1974), *Adv. Protein Chem.*, **28**, 1-210.
[66]   Tullins, T. D., Frank, P. *et al.* (1978), *P. N. A. S.*, **75**, 4069-73.
[67]   Vallee, B. and Williams, R. J. P. (1968), *P. N. A. S.*, **59**, 498-505.
[68]   Walker, G. A., Murphy, S., *et al.* (1969), *Arch. Biochem. Biophys.* **134**, 95-102.
[69]   Webb, J., *et al.* (1973), *Biochemistry*, **12**, 1797-802.
[70]   Weinberg, E. D. (1970), *Adv. microbial Physiol.*, 4, 1-44.
[71]   Watterson, D. M., Van Eldik, L., *et al.* (1976), *P. N. A. S.*, **73**, 2711-5.
[72]   Williams, R. J. P. (1970), *Quart. Revs. chem. Soc.*, **24**, 331-65.
[73]   Williams, R. J. P. (1972), *Physiol. chem. Phys.*, **4**, 427-39.
[74]   Zabinski, R., Munck, E. *et al.* (1972), *Biochemistry*, **11**, 3212-9.

Index

Compounds are shown with physiologically associated metals or co-factors in parentheses.